A Tour of Reconstruction

New Directions in Southern History

The Lost State of Franklin: America's First Secession
Kevin T. Barksdale

Bluecoats and Tar Heels: Soldiers and Civilians in Reconstruction North Carolina
Mark L. Bradley

Becoming Bourgeois: Merchant Culture in the South, 1820–1865
Frank J. Byrne

Cowboy Conservatism: Texas and the Rise of the Modern Right
Sean P. Cunningham

A Tour of Reconstruction: Travel Letters of 1875
Anna Dickinson (J. Matthew Gallman, ed.)

Raising Racists: The Socialization of White Children in the Jim Crow South
Kristina DuRocher

Lum and Abner: Rural America and the Golden Age of Radio
Randal L. Hall

The New Southern University: Academic Freedom and Liberalism at UNC
Charles J. Holden

Entangled by White Supremacy: Reform in World War I–era South Carolina
Janet G. Hudson

Cultivating Race: The Expansion of Slavery in Georgia, 1750–1860
Watson W. Jennison

The View from the Ground: Experiences of Civil War Soldiers
edited by Aaron Sheehan-Dean

Reconstructing Appalachia: The Civil War's Aftermath
edited by Andrew L. Slap

Blood in the Hills: A History of Violence in Appalachia
edited by Bruce E. Stewart

Moonshiners and Prohibitionists: The Battle over Alcohol in Southern Appalachia
Bruce E. Stewart

Southern Farmers and Their Stories: Memory and Meaning in Oral History
Melissa Walker

Law and Society in the South: A History of North Carolina Court Cases
John W. Wertheimer

A TOUR OF

Reconstruction

Travel Letters of 1875

ANNA DICKINSON

EDITED BY

J. MATTHEW GALLMAN

THE UNIVERSITY PRESS OF KENTUCKY

Scholarly publisher for the Commonwealth,
serving Bellarmine University, Berea College, Centre College of Kentucky, Eastern Kentucky University, The Filson Historical Society, Georgetown College, Kentucky Historical Society, Kentucky State University, Morehead State University, Murray State University, Northern Kentucky University, Transylvania University, University of Kentucky, University of Louisville, and Western Kentucky University.

Editorial and Sales Offices: The University Press of Kentucky
663 South Limestone Street, Lexington, Kentucky 40508-4008
www.kentuckypress.com

Frontispiece: Undated *carte de visite* of Anna Dickinson, copied from an original photograph by Napoleon Sarony, who ran a popular New York City studio. The portrait was probably made shortly after the Civil War. Unless otherwise noted, photographs are from J. Matthew Gallman's personal collection.

15 14 13 12 11   5 4 3 2 1

Library of Congress Cataloging-in-Publication Data

Dickinson, Anna E. (Anna Elizabeth), 1842-1932.
A tour of Reconstruction : travel letters of 1875 / Anna Dickinson ; edited by J. Matthew Gallman.
p. cm. – (New directions in southern history)
Includes bibliographical references and index.
ISBN 978-0-8131-3424-6 (hardcover : alk. paper) – ISBN 978-0-8131-3425-3 (ebook)
1. Dickinson, Anna E. (Anna Elizabeth), 1842-1932–Correspondence. 2. Dickinson, Anna E. (Anna Elizabeth), 1842-1932–Travel–Southern States. 3. Reconstruction (U.S. history, 1865-1877)–Sources. 4. Southern States–Social conditions–19th century–Sources. 5. Southern States–Economic conditions–19th century–Sources. I. Gallman, J. Matthew (James Matthew) II. Title.
E668.D547 2011
975'.04–dc23   2011024138

This book is printed on acid-free paper meeting the requirements of the American National Standard for Permanence in Paper for Printed Library Materials.

Manufactured in the United States of America.

Member of the Association of American University Presses

CONTENTS

ACKNOWLEDGMENTS

This project has been somewhere in the back of my mind since I first read Dickinson's 1875 letters while preparing a biographical study of her life. At that time, I prepared a rough transcription of these letters to use in my own research. Even then, I thought they would make a wonderful book and a valuable teaching tool.

The problem was that among Anna Dickinson's many virtues, good penmanship was sadly absent. For many years, the book sat on the back burner. Periodically, when fate or good fortune presented me with a research assistant, I would set my researcher to work transcribing the letters (or improving upon the previous effort). Thanks to Christina Ericson Hansen, Holly Fisher, Angela Diaz, and Jennifer Lyon, who each took a crack at unraveling Dickinson's handwriting. Jennifer also made the first pass at writing the endnotes. Needless to say, I made all the final calls on the transcription and notes.

As I was preparing the manuscript for publication, many colleagues offered support and good advice. Thanks to Meredith Babb for providing valuable encouragement at the early stages of the project. Michael Fitzgerald offered some wise counsel on Reconstruction. Michele Gillespie and the two anonymous readers for the University Press of Kentucky helped shape the introduction and the explanatory notes. Michele and her fellow series editors,

ACKNOWLEDGMENTS

Bill Link and Pete Carmichael—three of the best in the business—gave this project their stamp of approval and helped steer it through the publication process. Anne Dean Watkins and her colleagues at the University Press of Kentucky have been wonderful, and far more organized and professional than their too-harried author/editor.

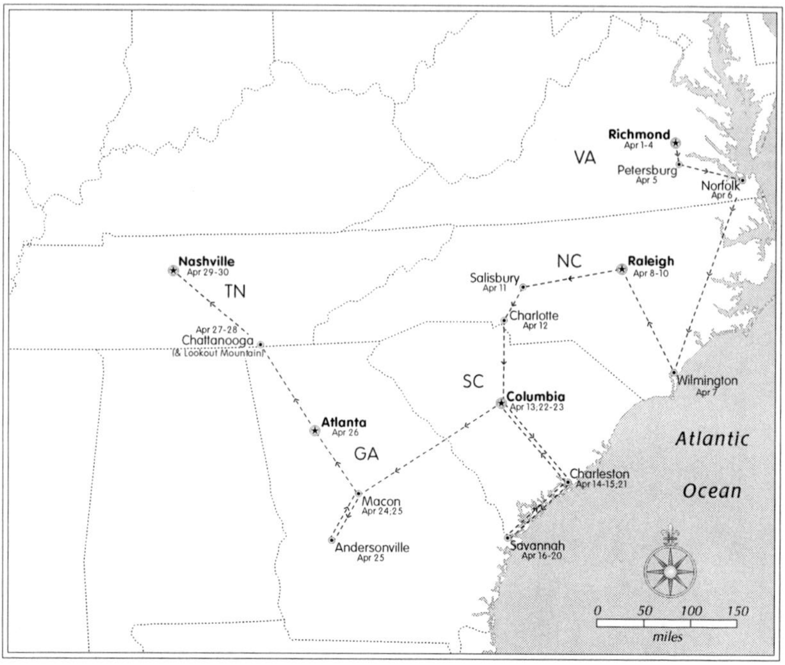

Anna Dickinson's 1875 route (Dick Gilbreath, University of Kentucky Cartography Lab)

Anna Dickinson's Itinerary

These are the places Dickinson visited and spent each night during her tour in 1875. She lectured in nearly every location.

April 1–4	Richmond, Virginia
April 5	Petersburg, Virginia
April 6	Norfolk, Virginia
April 7	Wilmington, North Carolina
April 8–10	Raleigh, North Carolina
April 11	Salisbury, North Carolina
April 12	Charlotte, North Carolina
April 13	Columbia, South Carolina
April 14–15	Charleston, South Carolina
April 16–20	Savannah, Georgia
April 21	Charleston, South Carolina
April 22–23	Columbia, South Carolina
April 24	Macon, Georgia
April 25	Andersonville, Georgia (returned to Macon that night)
April 26	Atlanta, Georgia
April 27–28	Chattanooga, Tennessee (and Lookout Mountain)
April 29–30	Nashville, Tennessee

INTRODUCTION

In late March 1875, popular orator Anna Dickinson set off from Washington, D.C., for an extended tour of the Reconstruction South. Dickinson was a professional public speaker who had arranged her itinerary in search of paying audiences, but she was also anxious to see what the South looked like a decade after Appomattox. Fortunately for us, she took copious notes and sent long letters home describing what she saw. Few moments in American history would be more interesting to visit than the South in 1875. And few observers could match Anna Dickinson's critical eye and caustic wit. The result is a marvelous portrait of a Southern world in flux and a strong-willed Northern woman clinging to her own fame.

Anna Dickinson was born in Philadelphia in 1842. Her abolitionist father died when she was an infant, so Dickinson was raised by her Quaker mother in a household with four older siblings. The precocious Quaker grew up admiring abolitionists like William Lloyd Garrison, Wendell Phillips, and Lucretia Mott. When she was fourteen, Dickinson published a letter in Garrison's abolitionist newspaper, the *Liberator.* On the eve of the Civil War, she stood up at a public meeting on women's rights and delivered an impromptu address, sparking her taste for public speaking. Before long, the fiery young orator was entertaining invitations to speak to abolitionist and women's rights au-

diences across the Philadelphia region. Garrison was so impressed with Dickinson's early efforts that he helped arrange a series of paid engagements for her in the Boston area. It did not take long for savvy Republican operatives to conclude that this charismatic young woman had a gift for moving audiences and a passion for the Union cause. By the time she was twenty-one years old, Anna Dickinson was a bona fide celebrity.[1]

Between 1863 and 1875, Anna Dickinson was one of America's most well-known public women. She spent six months and more each year on the road, traveling from town to town delivering lectures on abolitionism, politics and public affairs, and women's rights. During the Civil War, she was a powerful radical voice supporting the Union and pushing Abraham Lincoln to move further and faster on abolitionism and equal rights. After the war Dickinson did her best to parlay her wartime fame into an income as a lyceum speaker. A passionate advocate for women, she spoke on suffrage, prostitution, polygamy, and the rights of working women. While many of her competitors on the lyceum circuit opted for light entertainment, Dickinson tackled the thorny social issues of the day, including compulsory education and penitentiary reform. But while she produced highly topical new material each season, Dickinson also entertained her audiences with her popular lecture on the life and times of Joan of Arc.[2]

By all accounts, Dickinson was a spellbinding speaker. The diminutive Quaker with the short-cropped dark curls

---

Opposite: This *carte de visite* was taken of Dickinson at Wilson Brothers Studio in Hartford, Connecticut. It is undated but was probably taken during the Civil War. Dickinson was a frequent visitor to Hartford, where she spent time with woman's rights advocate Isabella Beecher Hooker and author and editor Charles Dudley Warner and his wife, Susan.

would pace up and down the stage like a caged lion, speaking without notes for an hour or more, in a powerful voice that easily reached the most distant corners of crowded lecture halls. During the Civil War, when she was still in her early twenties, Dickinson enraptured and scandalized audiences by exchanging barbs with antiwar hecklers and generally pushing beyond the expected bounds of proper female behavior.[3] After the war, she exchanged her staid Quaker garments for more fashionable garb. A savvy businesswoman, she cultivated her national fame and her particular identity as the young patriotic heroine of the Civil War. The nation's leading photographers clamored to take her picture, and her fans purchased small *cartes de visite* to place in their photo albums.[4] Others—particularly young women—wrote to her seeking autographs, locks of hair, or simply advice.

Few Americans of her day spent as much time on the road as Anna Dickinson. By her early thirties, she was on friendly terms with many of the railroad conductors working the lines up and down the East Coast and in much of the Midwest. On several occasions, she ventured farther west, speaking and touring in Colorado and northern California. An avid adventurer, Dickinson was credited as the first white woman to surmount Colorado's Long's Peak. By the time she was in her early twenties, Dickinson had grown accustomed to the amenities offered by the nation's most luxurious urban hotels, and when she ventured into smaller towns she expected the best rooms they had to offer. Wherever she roamed, fellow travelers clamored for her attention. She often complained in letters home about nosy strangers disturbing her privacy, but most in these Northern cities and towns were adoring fans. In many senses, for the proud Republican loyalist an excursion into the old Confederacy promised a very different sort of experience.

After 1870, cabinet cards replaced *cartes de visite* as the most popular photographic format. This picture was taken in Napoleon Sarony's New York studio, probably around the time of Dickinson's southern tour.

The decision to venture into the South in 1875 reflected some combination of economic necessity and unbridled curiosity. After the economic crisis of 1873, the lyceum circuit had fallen into decline. Crowds dwindled, and invitations to speak dried up. For some lecturers, this simply meant that they returned to other vocations. But for over a decade Dickinson had been dependent on her lecture earning, and—worse—her mother and older sister relied on her for financial support. Perhaps she could find paying audiences among those Southerners who had never had the opportunity to see the likes of Anna Dickinson in person. Meanwhile, a tour of the defeated South would give Dickinson a chance to see the progress of Reconstruction for herself, hopefully providing fodder for future writing. Once she had committed to the venture, Dickinson set her friend and occasional agent New Yorker O. W. Bernard the task of arranging a tour. Although she often traveled alone or with a female companion, for this extended tour Dickinson would travel with Bernard as her manager and periodic protector. He would make arrangements with suitable houses, contact the local press, handle travel reservations, and often run the ticket booth on the day of a lecture.

Although it was certainly an intriguing plan, the tour had its share of financial risks. A decade after the Civil War, the Southern economy continued to struggle. Even if her hosts proved enthusiastic, would Dickinson sell enough tickets to cover their expenses? And would Dickinson's fame, which had now spread throughout the South, translate into enthusiastic audiences? In 1875, there were still relatively few women who engaged in the sort of public speaking that was Dickinson's stock in trade, and most of those concentrated their energies in the North. Dickinson's very identity seemed to challenge Southern notions of womanhood. Would Southern audiences pay to hear such a woman—even a famous celebrity—speak in public? Moreover, she had made her reputation as a fierce defender of the Union during the Civil War. In 1875 many Americans still associated her with the bloody conflict. How would Southern audiences respond to a visitor so deeply aligned with the conquering North?

Dickinson had long been a particularly outspoken advocate of abolition and civil rights for African Americans. During the war, some of her most eloquent rhetoric had celebrated the heroism of the men of the U.S. Colored Troops. In the immediate postwar years, she broke ranks with her woman suffrage colleagues by supporting black manhood suffrage. In 1868 she had published a controversial novel, *What Answer?* featuring a tragic interracial marriage. How would a woman of such convictions fare in the Reconstruction South?

It certainly was an interesting time for such a tour. In June 1865 Dickinson and her family had visited Richmond and Petersburg for a few days, leaving her with vivid memories of the war's destruction. Now, ten years later, the old Confederate states were still struggling with the material and psychological impact of four years of bloody warfare and a devastating defeat. Moreover, the Southern states continued to wrestle with the cultural, economic, and political implications of emancipation. How would blacks and whites navigate this reconstituted biracial world? Who would have access to political office? To schools? To public places? How would the reconstructed states organize their judicial and penal systems? How would these largely agrarian states, for so long dependent on slave labor, organize themselves economically? And, hovering over all of these questions, how would the individual Southern states interact with the federal government and the victorious North?

The ten years since Dickinson's last visit had seen an immense amount of experimentation, controversy, and violence, as the reconstructed South navigated this terrain.

Scholars commonly present Reconstruction in three chronological periods, framed largely by the role of the federal government in the political drama. In practice, these years unfolded very differently in different states and communities, but the traditional framework is a useful way of making preliminary sense of a complex narrative.[5]

Discussions about how to reconstruct the postwar South began long before the war had ended, as northern radicals and moderates sparred over what sort of terms to offer to entice the Rebel states back into the Union. In December 1863, Abraham Lincoln issued his "10 percent plan," offering the states in rebellion a fairly easy path back to national statehood. Radicals, Dickinson among them, found Lincoln's terms too generous and called on the president to place more substantial conditions on the vanquished Confederates. These wartime debates underscored a fundamental uncertainty: once the war had ended, what branch of government would control the nation's future? Following Lincoln's assassination, coming on the heels of Gen. Robert E. Lee's surrender at Appomattox Court House in April 1865, newly sworn-in President Andrew Johnson asserted the power of the executive branch. With Congress out of session until that December, the Unionist Democrat from Tennessee stole a march on the Radical Republicans in Congress by paving the way for the smooth and relatively painless return of the Rebel states to the Union. Under Johnson's terms, the Confederate states had to repeal secession and accept emancipation, and their military and political leaders had to apply for individual pardons, but Johnson gave no indication that the federal government would interfere much with the internal politics of individual states or with the political and economic fates of the Southern freedpeople. Before long, Southern white Democrats had acted to solidify control over their states, passing harsh black codes to control freedpeople while repeatedly returning their old leaders to political office.

This initial period of Presidential Reconstruction did not last long. Reports of unrepentant Southern whites and violence against ex-slaves outraged Northern voters, who sent a cohort of Radical Republicans to Congress intent on wresting power from the embattled Johnson. In a series of acts beginning in March 1867, Congress overturned Johnson's Reconstruction measures and carved the old Confederacy into ten military districts, pending the acceptance of new state constitutions guaranteeing—among other things—black manhood suffrage. In the meantime, Union soldiers would remain as an armed government force in the region, while federal agents in the Freedmen's Bureau were to act to protect the interests of the freedpeople. These measures began a decade that scholars have termed Congressional or Radical Reconstruction.

For a time, black voters had tremendous political power across the South, as many Southern whites were either disenfranchised by the Reconstruction Acts or refused to participate in this revolutionary political system. Coalitions of black voters, Southern white Unionists, and white Republicans from the North dominated state constitutional conventions, crafting new and often innovative constitutions that suggested a brave new world of interracial politics and economic development. In states like South Carolina, where African Americans were in the majority, black voters sent black representatives to the state legislature in substantial numbers. Elsewhere, coalitions of black voters and white Republicans controlled state and local governments at least for a time. Once they had been readmitted to the Union, these Republican coalitions set about the complicated business of creating a new institutional infrastructure while attempting to rebuild the ravaged Southern economy. States built new penitentiaries and experimented with penal reform. Integrated schools brought whites and blacks together in the same classrooms. Some state legislatures encouraged railroad building and industrial investment.

Each Southern state had its own political and demographic composition, and thus events unfolded in different ways in different settings, but by 1875 broad patterns had emerged and for many the high hopes of Reconstruction had long since been dashed. White Democrats in most states had made major strides in regaining political control of the state governments, conspiring to disenfranchise freedmen through legislative chicanery and raw violence and intimidation. Republican governments, where they survived, grew increasingly embattled. Meanwhile, the cash-poor postwar agricultural economy grew dependent on an inefficient and demoralizing system of sharecropping.

For freedpeople, the transition to freedom produced mixed results. Emancipation certainly brought its own immense rewards, as families separated by slavery came together in autonomous households and black communities created a vibrant institutional world of churches, political organizations, militia groups, and voluntary societies. Most ex-slaves continued to work the land, in many cases the very same soil they had toiled on in slavery, but now they largely farmed small plots. Gone were the large plantations of the antebellum years. But only a fortunate few were able to save enough money to purchase their own farms; most worked the land as sharecroppers, fortunate if they could cover their accumulated debts at the end of each growing season.[6] With emancipation had come grand hopes for new generations of black youth no longer deprived of formal education. Here, too, the record was mixed. Literacy among Southern black children increased remarkably in the postwar decades, but education for African Americans still lagged well behind that for Southern whites and that in the Northern states.[7]

The year 1877 traditionally marks the end of Reconstruction. Following his controversial election in 1876, Ohio Republican Rutherford B. Hayes ordered the final federal troops removed from the South, effectively leaving Southern white Democrats in political control of most of the old Confederacy. By the time Dickinson and Bernard ventured into the South in 1875, many Northern voters had already lost their enthusiasm for Reconstruction. Northerners who had been enthusiastic about producing a reformed South free of the vestiges of slavery and secession had long since grown weary of reports of violence, corruption, and economic decay. Meanwhile, corruption and financial crisis closer to home had undermined Northern enthusiasm for a costly ongoing federal presence in the South.

In 1872, a coalition of Republicans disenchanted with President Ulysses S. Grant bolted the party to support the *New York Tribune*'s Horace Greeley in his bid for the presidency as head of a newly formed Liberal Republican Party. Greeley, once an outspoken abolitionist, called for the North and South to "clasp hands across the bloody chasm" and return the South to "self rule." Dickinson, responding to both personal loyalties and political ideology, had cast her lot with Greeley and given several highly publicized stump speeches for the Liberal Republicans. Black Southerners had already won the vote, she argued, and thus "before the law they stand on a level with the whitest white man." "If they cannot defend themselves and exercise their right at the polls," then we should either accept that the war had never really been won or "confess the Republican Union is ended." In a sense, this was a disingenuous argument, designed to appeal to white Northern voters who would welcome any excuse to turn their backs on Southern blacks. But Dickinson had honestly come to believe that the South's future depended on the actions of Southerners—both white and black—as opposed to interventions from the North.[8] Her journey to the South a few years later presented an opportunity to assess the state of things with her own eyes.

As chance would have it, Dickinson and Bernard headed south at a particularly interesting moment. Shortly before the intrepid pair set off, President Ulysses S. Grant signed the Civil Rights Act of 1875 into law. This legislation, authored by Dickinson's hero Massachusetts senator Charles Sumner, guaranteed equal access to public accommodations—hotels, restaurants, trains, lecture halls—regardless of race, color, or previous condition of servitude. Establishments that refused to follow this new federal law were subject to fines of $500 or more. This, in turn, meant that white proprietors faced with black guests would have to choose between paying huge fines and alienating their white customers. Nobody really knew how the law would work in practice. Would blacks demand their newly won access to public spaces? Would whites acquiesce or resist? Would the federal government really have the wherewithal to enforce the law? In practice, the Civil Rights Act proved to be more smoke than substance. The federal courts largely left it to black citizens to file complaints, and few fines were ever levied. But for the brief period when Dickinson was on tour the question remained open, and many proprietors elected to take the law seriously.[9]

Dickinson and Bernard left Washington for Richmond, Virginia, on April 1, 1875. Over the next month, they wound their way through Virginia, North Carolina, South Carolina, Georgia, and Tennessee. In addition to Richmond, Dickinson visited and lectured in Petersburg, Wilmington, Raleigh, Charlotte, Charleston, Savannah, Nashville, and various small towns. Her travels did not take her through the Deep South, which had witnessed some of Reconstruction's most bloody scenes, but she did observe a wide array of political and economic circumstances.[10] In Virginia, Democrats had long since regained control of the state by forming a coalition with some moderate Republicans. Although a few black representatives remained in Virginia's statehouse, Dickinson observed a political culture dominated by white Democrats and steeped in Confederate traditions. In North Carolina and Georgia, Republican governments had long since given way to Democratic "Redeemers." In the immediate postwar years, Tennessee had been a bastion of Unionist sentiment, but by the mid-1870s Southern Democrats had achieved dominance in Andrew Johnson's home state. In each of these states, Dickinson would note differences in the status of blacks, the state of the economy, and the overall attitudes of the people she met, but in all cases white Democrats held the political reins of power. South Carolina was a different story. Supported by a black voting majority, the Republican Party still maintained a tenuous political majority in 1875. In 1874 the state had elected onetime Massachusetts abolitionist Daniel Chamberlain as governor, on the promise of sweeping reforms after years of corruption. Chamberlain, the brother of Dickinson's friend and former suitor Leander Chamberlain, had charted a course that seemed designed to appease his Democratic adversaries while maintaining his core support.

Each state held its own fascinations for Dickinson. Particularly attuned to remnants of the Civil War, she made a point to tour the battlefields near Petersburg, Charleston, and Chattanooga, and the sites of wartime prisoner-of-war camps in Richmond; Andersonville, Georgia; and Salisbury, North Carolina. Always fascinated by architecture and monuments, whenever she stayed in a state capital, Dickinson visited the statehouse, commenting—often quite critically—on the condition of the buildings and grounds. As she and Bernard spent hundreds of hours in trains crisscrossing the South, Dickinson inventoried the state of agriculture, farm buildings, trees, and even the soil they passed over. And wherever they ventured, Dickinson observed her surroundings with a particular eye to how Reconstruction was unfolding.

In a dozen years of travels, Anna Dickinson was always a devoted correspondent with her mother, Mary Dickinson, who Anna called "Marmee." But these 1875 letters to Mary Dickinson are not exactly like Dickinson's familiar correspondence home. They are in fact more similar to the long letters Dickinson wrote from a subsequent western tour, which became the basis of her popular travel book, *A Ragged Register*.[11] It seems clear that although Dickinson addressed her 1875 letters to her mother, she really saw this correspondence as a written record of her journeys for posterity. Each of the four exceedingly long letters includes a narrative of roughly a week on the road. And whereas Dickinson's normal letters were full of routine news and comments about family and friends, these letters barely mention personal topics. As they periodically indicate, Dickinson also used these mailings as an opportunity to mail materials home. Sometimes she picked a flower or a sprig from a plant. More often she sent home a newspaper story describing her latest lecture. None of these added materials is filed among her correspondence, but she included some of the clippings in her extensive scrapbooks.[12]

For the scholar and student, Dickinson's 1875 letters offer a treasure of commentary and observation about the postwar South. The letters have many valuable and intriguing aspects, but three overarching traits stand out. First, Dickinson was no passive observer. She had a knack for asking interesting and important questions about what she saw and for seeking out black and white Southerners across the spectrum to discuss the issues of the day. She was particularly interested in unpacking the multiple ways the legacy of the Civil War continued to shape the worlds she visited. Time and again, she turned her analytic eye to the state of race relations and the status of African Americans in the reconstructed South. How were blacks and whites granted access to education? What did white legislators do when they needed the votes of elected black officials? Were the men on the chain gangs disproportionately black? Dickinson was particularly attuned to the local responses to interlopers from the North. Did educators or clergy betray their Northern roots? How were local citizenry responding to politicians from the North? What were the best models to improve Southern institutions for both races without alienating those white Southerners who were destined to hold the reins of power? Few casual observers would have been as sensitive to these racial and regional dynamics. Dickinson's observations and commentaries are an excellent illustration of how a radical abolitionist viewed the South ten years after the war.

Following pages: Throughout her tour, Dickinson attracted tremendous attention from the local press. She routinely clipped newspaper stories—both positive reports and the angry attacks—and included them in her letters to her mother. The letters periodically make reference to these accounts and her ongoing verbal battles with local editors. After she returned home, Dickinson added these clippings to her voluminous scrapbooks. These are portions of pages from those books. (Library of Congress)

St Lo[illegible]

Daily Democrat.

SATURDAY MORNING. MAY 8, 1875.

ANNA DICKINSON.

How She Looked and Talked at Mercantile Library Last Night.

Miss Anna Dickinson, one of the most eloquent and winning of the professional lecturers on woman suffrage, lectured last night at the Mercantile Library to a small and select audience, her subject being "A Woman's Opinion of It." In token, perhaps, of her faith, Miss Dickinson wore suspended on her bosom a gold cross, which, with the chain around her throat, appeared an agreeable set off to a beautiful black silk dress fitting close to the throat, and made more elegant by a heavy overskirt of black lace. At the throat and at the cuffs of the sleeves was an edging of white lace, which again lined the sleeves, barred at the back, and cut so as to leave her arms free to gesticulate at pleasure. Diamond drops glittered from her ears, and a solitaire ring sparkled from the fourth finger of her left hand. Surmounting the quick, firm, elastic figure was a strong head, with black hair cut short, in Quaker fashion, and massed at the temples over the low, broad, white forehead. Beneath the forehead glanced a pair of earnest, deep-set eyes, so far sheltered beneath the brow that their color could not, at first, be distinctly seen. On the cheek could be seen, at times, a rich roseate hue, too fresh and transitory to be mistaken for the effect of cosmetic—a face that would be beautiful in its outlines if it were not for the rather long and prominent jaw. But all observation of this physical defect was swept away when she entered fairly upon her lecture. The magic of her tones and the sweetness and eloquence of her words, spoken, evidently, with strong feeling on her part, cannot be transferred to paper.

Passing by the questions of the day—the Louisiana difficulties, the Arkansas problem, the financial difficulties of the country, the third term—she spoke of a question affecting not a section or an age, but one as old as sorrow and suffering and sin, and as widespread as humanity—an evil whose boughs spread abroad, dropping their poisonous growth across all the land. She referred to the mooted propriety of discussing such evils to say that cowardice was not necessarily delicacy, nor selfishness refinement of feeling, and [illegible] in the press, on the stage, in the novels of the day, [illegible] [illegible] was revealed without the truth underlying it, and in sermons it was hinted at without any sermon on the truth lying beyond it. She then took up the real subject of her lecture: The prejudiced, Italian sentiment of society which holds a woman's venial fault to be a mortal crime, and a man's mortal crime to be but a venial fault. She inveighed eloquently against the idea that in remorseless, heartless, soulless dissipation young men were merely sowing wild oats, which they must sow to come to manhood; whereas, every one knew that it was destruction to the heaven of a happy girlhood, an honorable womanhood, a dignified and noble wifehood and motherhood, and would produce sorrow, remorse, degradation and anguish. She combatted the idea that woman's fall was necessarily so much greater because of the greater height from which she falls. On the idea that "for a man to fall affects but himself alone, and himself so slightly," she rung the changes with terrible sarcasm; so far from it, eight-tenths of all the sorrow, misery, degradation, sin and crime in civilized communities she held to be the outgrowth of this false conception. She inveighed vehemently against the blasphemy of the conception that prostitution was a necessary evil, which, in fact, was nothing but a deliberate assertion that God had created beings to be given over to an absolute destruction of body and soul, as a necessity for the preservation [illegible] and the race. 760

In conclusion, Miss Dickinson appealed for a change in public sentiment which would teach that a man's manhood can only be honorable and complete by being as complete and as sweet as a woman's woman good. [Applause.]

Anna Dickinson will tell us to-night what she knows about her ancient sister, Joan of Arc, who put on masculine breeches, and got into trouble by it. How about Mrs. Mary Dr. Walker? 761

We regret that our friend and *confrere*, Jos. P. Caldwell, has been confined to his room for the past fortnight by a severe

---

The Southern Home:

Office over Burwell, Grier & Co.'s Store Corner of Fourth and Tryon Streets.

MONDAY, APRIL 12, 1875.

A writer in the *Observer* urges our people to go to hear Anna Dickinson, the notorious female Rightist, at the Opera House to night. We trust our true people, who value modesty and womanly decorum will do no such thing. Without casting any particular imputation against the private character of Miss Dickinson, it is a fact not to be denied that she is one of the foremost of those women shriekers, whose doctrines or "isms" have done so much to unhinge and demoralize even the best Northern society. It should be remembered that Miss Dickinson has never been a friend of the South, but, on the contrary, only recently, (if we mistake not) joined in an address wherein the Radical party was incidently censured for not going greater lengths in Radicalizing our section. The Salisbury *Watchman* hits the nail on the head as follows:

"We regard such interlopers as forerunners of evil. When we consider what has followed the lectures of the so-called strong minded women in the North, we cannot but regard them as public pests. The true lady cannot assume such a *role*, and aside from the unnatural and immoral aspect of the case, such conduct is to be deplored, and ought not to be countenanced by good people. 762

The Daily Journal

THURSDAY, MAY 6, 1875.

ANNA DICKINSON.

The second appearance of Miss Dickinson in this city last evening was a flattering ovation. The Opera House was quite full, and the audience was unanimous in its verdict of approval and admiration for the talented woman. "A Woman's Opinion of It" was her view of the different codes by which erring women and men are judged, and the general influence and effect of the social evil. Miss Dickinson attempted difficult ground here, for there can be but one dispassionate view of the question, and this she took—that men and women should be held responsible alike by society. Miss Dickinson's difficulty was in upholding her oratorical and literary fame without advancing any original thought. To say that she succeeded brilliantly, will be borne out with us by the refined audience. Her metaphors and illustrations were chosen as delicately as she would choose flowers from a bed, and the audience testified its unqualified delight by frequent and hearty applause, and the effort was more generally appreciated than the former. 763

Miss Dickinson goes hence to St. Louis, and thence to the Pacific slope, where we doubt not her fame will be added to as it deserves.

MISS ANNA E. DICKINSON proposes to deliver a lecture in Savannah before a great while on a subject not yet announced. Our exchanges state that she has approached the public on "The Social Evil" in the North with considerable effect. It is quite possible for a virtuous female to theorize on such a subject, but when she attempts to lecture the public, the public naturally looks for expressions arising from actual experience of the question presented. Hence the lecturer must have better knowledge of the subject than comports with elegant society, or she is ignorant of the matter she is to discuss. Our information points to no conclusion that the most [illegible] reader will not comprehend. 764

THE REPUBLICAN.

ST. LOUIS.

SATURDAY, MAY 8, 1875.

Anna Dickinson's Lecture Last Night.

A very slender audience gathered at the Mercantile Library hall last night to hear Anna Dickinson lecture. It was noticeable in the grouping of the audience that the ladies gathered pretty much in a bunch in the front seats while the sterner sex scattered itself out further back as though a little awed at the prospect of hearing "A Woman's opinion of It." The stage was perfectly bare, being unprovided with any desk or even chair by which the lecturer might gain some relief of position. A little after eight o'clock Miss Dickinson came for-

INDEX AND APPEAL.

MONDAY, APRIL 5, 1875.

ANNA DICKINSON.—On Monday evening, April 5th, Miss Dickinson will make her first and only appearance in this city at the Academy of Music. Her subject "Joan of Arc" is spoken of so highly by the Richmond press that we feel warranted in urging our citizens to assemble in force to welcome her. The Richmond *Dispatch*, which is slow to praise, pays the following compliment to this distinguished lady:

It was not at all surprising that Miss Dickinson should have a larger audience last night than the one which greeted her first appearance in this city. There were many persons present who had not heard her grand historic speech on Joan of Arc, and some went away—shall we say disappointed? It may be so; but they ought not to have been. The difference between the lecture What's to Hinder and Joan of Arc is so great that one would hardly imagine, having heard both, that they came from the same source. Miss Dickinson is not an advocate of woman's rights. She cannot be accused fairly of advocating any such thing.

It is true she is a politician; it is true that she once advocated the abolition of slavery; and it is equally true that she stumped the North in the last Presidential campaign against Grant, and to-day opposes the iniquities of the Civil Rights bill. Her mission to the South is not that of an enemy, but a friend. This was her avowal last night; and can it be doubted when it comes from the lips of a woman whose every word has been as chaste and as refined as the most fastidious in our midst could desire?

Anna Dickinson is beyond all doubt a pure-minded woman, and the record of her good deeds—which are nowhere disputed—attest the truth of this assertion. She is modest, retiring and graceful in her manner, and yet a striking-looking lady; and whatever may be the emotional feelings which possess her heart, there are many good traits in her character which are stamped upon her face, and which show themselves in the thoughts which she utters.

On the evening of her first lecture she wore a black silk dress with a Yak-lace over-dress. Her hair, which is jet black, was cut short, and curls hung prettily about her graceful head. She had on a pair of gold bands, and wore around her neck a gold chain, to which was attached a simple gold cross. Upon her left hand she wore two beautiful diamond rings, which sparkled and attracted the eyes of her audience, even if her personal appearance didn't. Last night she wore a beautiful black silk dress, which was fastened at the throat with a sparkling diamond breastpin.

Reserved seats can be secured at the office of the *Rural Messenger* and we advise an early application for seats. 736

THE DAILY NEWS.

THURSDAY..........APRIL 8, 1875.

MISS ANNA DICKINSON.—This lady appears before a Raleigh audience to-night, and we bespeak a full attendance and such a respectful hearing as the people of our city will be expected to give.

There has been a vast deal of misapprehension about this lady, and because she has appeared upon the rostrum as a lecturer, we have straightway assigned her to that pestilent class, the woman's righter, against which every womanly instinct revolts and before which the chivalric deference of manhood is thrown aside.

On the contrary she is an earnest intellectual woman, addressing herself with ardor to the subjects of the hour, working for the elevation of her race; again, as on her present tour dealing with subjects replete with historical interest and full of poetic associations.

We have pictured Miss Dickinson as a woman passed the middle age, tall, scrawny and gawky, hair defiant of fashion, hanging in tangled knots over a pair of fierce sparkling eyes, manner coarse, masculine and aggressive, and altogether such a one as would cause her a hostile reception.

On the contrary she is described as a person possessed of "extraordinary personal beauty, made up as it is of fine features, a skin with the clear creamy, and ruddy tints of the tea rose, black curling hair, dazzling teeth, and eyes like nothing so much as the *aqua marine* jewel, at once soft and brilliant to the last degree. She arrays this beauty after a style of quaint picturesqueness, never affronting fashion, nor yet subservient to it." 737

Now this is an attractive picture, and when to this is added a dramatic power which is compared to that of Ristori, we have reason to expect that her lecture will be densely attended.

Her subject here will be the Career and Character of Joan of Arc.

DAILY ENQUIRER.

SATURDAY MORNING..........APRIL 3, 1875

RICHMOND THEATRE—*What's to Hinder?*—Last night, despite the inclement weather, there was a fine audience, including a large number of our most fashionable people, at the theatre to hear Miss Anna Dickinson's second lecture, "What's to Hinder?" The substance of the lecture or speech—for she discards notes entirely—was that women should be educated and disciplined to meet the issues and exigencies of life upon the same principle that applies to men, and she supported her position by an argument, the principal force of which, is to be found in scenes of every day life familiar to all. Though some of the sentiments she uttered have seldom been heard in this community before, they were none the less true for that reason; and while her earnestness throughout was impassioned it must be confessed that her pictures were not over colored. Miss Dickinson advocates woman's rights in so far as they are embodied in her right to work, and to be able to take care of herself in the hour of adversity. She pleads the cause of woman from an elevated and noble standpoint, and whether the reformation she would work is practicable or not, no one can hear her and doubt her sincerity, or that the world would be better off if some of her theories were adopted. Her strictures upon society were in many respects but too full of point, and she held up the mirror for a portraiture that contained lessons none could study without benefit. Of Miss Dickinson's eloquence we have before spoken; it is of an order met with but seldom in a lifetime. We hope she will visit Richmond again at no distant day. 738

The Morning News

SATURDAY, APRIL 17, 1875.

"Joan of Arc"—Miss Anna Dickinson's Historical Sketch.

The audience that greeted Miss Anna Dickinson at the theatre last evening, upon her first appearance in this city, was remarkable for the large representation of the most intelligent and cultured portion of our community, embracing many prominent citizens and their families, who are rarely seen at the theatre unless some particularly notable entertainment is on the programme.

We were pleased to find that the high encomiums which have been bestowed upon Miss Dickinson by our Southern contemporaries were richly deserved, and that no exaggerated praise had been awarded her beautiful and eloquent historical sketch of "Joan of Arc."

The sight of a woman as a lecturer is a novel one for Southern audiences, and prejudice may have kept many from attending, but they will certainly regret it when they come to realize the truth of what will be told this morning and hear the verdict of her last night's audience.

She tells the story of the faithful peasant girl from her birth to her death so eloquently and grandly that one would imagine they were listening to the history of a great chieftain whose purity, gallant deeds, courageous fortitude, self-sacrificing spirit and untainted character were as indelibly imprinted upon our memory as the life and character of a Christian hero of our own day and generation.

She pictures in glowing terms the successes of her beautiful subject, and tells how she captures town after town, defeats the English in the open field, and routs the last remnant of the magnificent force sent to conquer her beloved France. Then the king is crowned, and that day crowns the life of the heroine with unspeakable happiness. Her work is completed. She begs that she may return to her own home, to her mother's sheltering care, where she may tend her father's flocks and pass her remaining days in quietude. But all to no purpose. The end comes at last. Her appeals are denied, and finally, through treachery, she falls into the power of her enemies. She is sold to the English, and at last it is fixed that she shall be burned.

Miss Dickinson concludes her powerful

Second, Dickinson had an impressive empirical eye and journalistic sensibilities. For the contemporary reader, it is striking how accurate her descriptions were. Her accounts of cemeteries, buildings, monuments, sculpture, prisoner-of-war camps, and the like are noteworthy for their careful attention to detail. The historian becomes accustomed to determining who were the more reliable witnesses. Judging from those physical descriptions that are subject to modern verification, Dickinson was a remarkably keen observer. The close reader will be rewarded with dozens of memorable images of buildings, landscapes, monuments, and everyday people who populated the upper South in 1875.

Finally, Dickinson's account of her trip is noteworthy because she was Anna Dickinson. That is, unlike the anonymous traveler-observer who blends into the background, Dickinson was a celebrated figure who attracted attention wherever she visited. Many white Southerners clearly associated her with the Union cause and the Civil War. Others saw her as a celebrity and a curiosity, particularly as a public woman whose routine behavior violated Southern gender norms. Local politicians quite wisely viewed Dickinson as a visitor who was assessing what she saw, with the intention of reporting back to Northern audiences. Time and again her hosts did their best to shape what she witnessed and the impressions she would take back with her.

Of course Dickinson did not approach her journeys as a dispassionate observer. The reader will quickly discover that she brought strong tastes and distinct biases with her as she toured. Ten years after Appomattox, the patriotic Dickinson was still in no mood to forgive the leaders of the Confederacy, and she did not care who knew it. Whereas other Northerners—including several of the travel writers who had gone before her—had embraced a spirit of reconciliation, when Dickinson walked the remains of battlefields and prisoner-of-war camps, the memories of the war remained fresh and her hostility to the Confederacy uncompromising. She also approached her travels as a devoted abolitionist who had long spoken for racial equality. On multiple occasions, she made it a point to visit black churches, chat with black citizens, and inquire about the state of race relations. Yet, her letters suggest that she was hardly free of the racial prejudice of her day. Dickinson spun humorous tales at the expense of the African Americans she observed, mocking their patterns of speech or lack of education. Nonetheless, she was clearly interested in social policies that would enhance the dignity and material conditions of Southern blacks.

Numerous themes run through these letters. In many senses, they fall within the familiar genre of the nineteenth-century travel narrative. European visitors and travelers from the North routinely toured the South both before and after the war, commenting on the people they encountered and the places they visited, while offering observations about the South's distinctive racial world. In the decades before the war, Alexis de Tocqueville, Harriet Martineau, Frederick Law Olmsted, and a host of others toured the plantation South, publishing their impressions.[13] Immediately after the war, journalist Whitelaw Reid—one of Dickinson's close friends—toured the conquered South with several members of the Johnson administration and published his observations in a widely distributed volume. Many others passed through the old Confederacy, offering their perspectives on this world in flux.[14]

As a veteran traveler of rather sophisticated tastes and limited patience, Dickinson's running commentary on hotels and trains, carriages, and other means of conveyance offer an entertaining window into the state of the postwar

South. The hotels and inns she visited ranged in quality, although the best certainly did not compare with the grand hotels she frequented in Chicago and New York. Many of Dickinson's most illuminating, and caustic, comments concern the ways her Southern hosts sought to cheat their Northern customers. Nothing annoyed her more than being charged for meals that she never requested and did not eat, or carriage rides to meet trains that were not coming, or newspaper ads in papers that proceeded to savage her in their editorials. Time and again, Dickinson recounts tales in which she and Bernard, often with a fellow Northern traveler, exchanged barbs with white Southerners who seemed intent on making an additional profit at the expense of the wealthy tourists.

It is striking how often Dickinson and Bernard stumbled upon some Northern traveling companion for some piece of their journey. This suggests something about the search for kindred spirits in a strange land, but it also illustrates the fact that many Northerners were drawn to the South either for business or pleasure. In fact, on several occasions Dickinson reported that she had run across some old friend. Her encounter with Henry Purvis, an African American friend from Philadelphia, provides a particularly interesting portrait of South Carolina's racial sensibilities. Although her hosts had seemed perfectly happy to accept Dickinson's presence in their midst, they could not tolerate her overly familiar chat with a black man. Other encounters, such as her brief visit with sculptor Emma Stebbins in Norfolk, illustrate a pattern that ran through much of Dickinson's life: wherever she traveled, she was a part of a vast network of celebrated public women, including actresses, artists, authors, journalists, reformers, and fellow lecturers. Even when she had little personally in common with these women, there seemed to be some bond that came with being a public woman in a world still skeptical of all such gender transgressors.

If Dickinson had particular experience with trains and hotels, she owed much of her professional stature to the attention and support she had received from the nation's press. For years she had counted many of the North's most powerful newspaper editors among her friends. Her letters offer a valuable portrait of the Southern newspapermen she encountered along the way. Wise in the ways of public opinion, these editors and their fellow civic leaders did their best to leave Dickinson with positive perceptions of their communities. Often Dickinson noted that her audiences were full of the "best people" of the town, who behaved politely and appeared genuinely happy to hear her. When it seemed that she might stray into unflattering places—such as Salisbury's prison camp with its long unmarked burial trenches—the locals did their best to discourage her curiosity (a strategy Dickinson quickly saw through). Sometimes she challenged her audiences, as when she called for compulsory universal education for both blacks and whites. Privately, she reported, the local elites would praise the merits of her arguments, but the next day the papers would be disappointingly silent. In fact, her repeated observations about stories that did not make the local papers are a discouraging cautionary tale for the historian who relies on newspaper evidence.

For the historian of women, these letters are thick with valuable anecdotes and observations. On several occasions Dickinson sought out those southern women who had been staunch Unionists during the war or who had at least made efforts to assist the Union prisoners in their midst. The most remarkable was certainly Richmond's Elizabeth Van Lew. During the war Van Lew had remained loyal to the Union, acting as an occasional spy while doing her best to assist Richmond's prisoners of war.[15] In Richmond, Van Lew took the traveling orator under her wing, producing some wonderful exchanges between two of the nation's most intriguing public women. When she visited South Carolina, Dickinson enjoyed meeting with Governor Chamberlain's wife, Alice. Mrs. Chamberlain offered a fascinating glimpse into the social isolation that even the wife of the governor endured when she came from the North.

Many of Dickinson's most entertaining passages concerned her encounters with those Southern women who immediately disliked her and everything she stood for. Scholars have noted the role of white women in supporting the Confederate cause during the war and in keeping the memory of the Lost Cause alive into the postwar decades. Time and again, Dickinson reported sparring with Southern women for whom the scars of war had never healed. "The women hate me & wont come to hear me," she reported from Richmond. In Savannah she stumbled into a verbal dustup with several women when she spoke of "Lee" rather than giving the revered general his full title. In Raleigh, Dickinson and Bernard stayed at the fashionable Tarboro house. The landlord was a Confederate veteran but "a *really* well disposed reconstructed man." His wife was another matter. Although she seemed "as sweet as honey" to their faces, Dickinson overheard her hostess declaring, "I'd like to see every wretch of a Yankee burned at the stake." These strong-minded women hardly match our notions of the idealized "Southern lady." They were the true keepers of the Lost Cause, honoring the Confederate dead and revering their surviving generals, every bit as much as Dickinson honored the Union's fallen soldiers and recalled Lee and his ilk as traitors to their country.[16]

This notion of competing memories of the Civil War runs through much of these letters. Even ten years after the war, Dickinson saw her own identity as firmly yoked to the Civil War and the Union cause. Since 1865, Dickinson had continued to trade on her wartime fame as America's Joan of Arc. Thus, it is no surprise that the memory of the war is so present in her own observations and commentary, particularly when her touring brought her face to face with evidence of the war's carnage. Although she was surely interested in assessing the contemporary state of the South, Dickinson missed no opportunity to tour a battlefield, prison camp, or federal cemetery. And, as it did for her Southern female antagonists, the memory of the war made Dickinson's blood boil as much in 1875 as thoughts of the Rebels had fired her angry rhetoric in the midst of the conflict.

Particularly striking for the historian are the myriad ways the white Southerners she met recalled and commemorated the war. These letters offer multiple glimpses into public rhetoric and ceremony intended to keep the Lost Cause alive. In private conversation, white Southerners routinely blamed their dire economic circumstances on the damage done by the Union army and the enduring legacy of a war for which they apparently—according to an exasperated Dickinson—accepted no responsibility. Time and again, she recorded scenes of gray-clad militia men or partisans marching under Confederate flags, with no U.S. flags anywhere in sight. Even though many Northerners had joined Greeley in calling on partisans from both regions to "clasp hands across the bloody chasm" of war, the Southern world Dickinson described in 1875 seemed one where the nerve endings were still quite raw and prospects for a happy reconciliation remote. This enduring Rebel passion clearly framed Dickinson's understanding of the South's future. Yet, the reader will note that her own regional hostilities are every bit as passionate as the most unreconstructed Southerner's. The bloody chasm apparently looked as deep from either side.[17]

Like many Northern observers, Dickinson was particularly anxious to assess the status of Southern blacks ten years after the war. Here her skills as an observer and researcher are particularly valuable. At each stop, Dickinson and Bernard would seek people to chat with on the street while planning investigative forays to schools, penitentiaries, factories and black churches. Occasionally, the new Civil Rights Act became the catalyst for conflict. In Wilmington, a well-dressed black man rejected a ticket in the traditionally black gallery and instead demanded a seat in the more expensive section of the hall, provoking cries of outrage from angry white patrons. Dickinson seemed unimpressed with this bold display, agreeing with those local blacks who told her that such maneuvers would merely bring white hostility upon their heads. Days before she arrived in Charlotte, North Carolina, her hotel had been the scene of a near riot when guests discovered a light-skinned black man—a member of the South Carolina state legislature—lodging in their midst. The hotelkeeper, no supporter of integration but unwilling to risk a $500 fine, managed to create a diversion so that the legislator and his family could flee in safety. Dickinson and Bernard witnessed no actual violence until they reached Nashville, where a mob broke into the local jail to lynch a black man who had killed a local policeman. "The man deserved hanging, no doubt," Dickinson concluded, but the whole affair was a "barbarous" violation of law and order. Ever alert to the power of the press, she noted that the local papers published a wildly distorted version of the episode that omitted the major role played by local leaders.

On many occasions, Dickinson applied her often idiosyncratic analytic gaze to Southern blacks in various everyday settings. Taken together, her comments present a fascinating portrait of how this radical abolitionist contemplated race in the postwar world. Clearly she remained true to her roots in advocating for racial justice in the South. Her letters are full of astute commentary on the unequal treatment of blacks in prisons or schools, and she appeared genuinely pleased with evidence of their economic or political successes. Yet she often employed a mocking tone toward her subjects that betrays her own biases. Thus, she visited a black church with Bernard only to regale her mother with a belittling account of the minister's error-filled sermon. In Norfolk she laughed at the inefficient "darkeys" who waited on her. No doubt these letters reveal a white observer who was not free of the prejudices of her time, but their author also seemed to judge both blacks and whites against the standard of her own vision of how Reconstruction should unfold. In Virginia she was particularly dissatisfied with the black church-goers who "must be like 'white folks'" while praising those freedpeople who remain true to their own cultural roots. In Petersburg she admired an orderly procession of black men and women, even though the local press mocked it as "a return to baffoonery," but then she joked about the new "colored cemetery" adjoining the white cemetery: "Why they should want to get so near the white people, dead, who hated & wronged them so living, is one of the problems."

As a careful observer, Dickinson was perpetually alert for opportunities to draw comparisons between Southern cities and states. Her comments often returned to how the various state governments had approached the challenges of Reconstruction. The white Virginians seem thoroughly unreconstructed when it comes to speeches and ceremonies recalling the Lost Cause, yet she noted that this state "without a carpet bag rule . . . had the sense to spend as much money & effort in behalf of the colored schools as of the white." In South Carolina she found whites refusing to attend integrated schools, yielding a probable future where there will be "a body of at least reasonably well informed colored people & of absolutely ignorant whites." And in Georgia she criticized the state for spending so little on schools, producing a class of ignorant blacks *and* poor whites.

Dickinson seemed most pleased with the freedpeople she encountered in South Carolina. In Charleston she saw "men & women, slaves ten years ago, who are not only well & elegantly dressed, but who carry themselves . . . with real—dignity & air of command" whereas elsewhere, and particularly in Georgia, "the manners of the darkies are very like those of slavery" with "a certain subdued almost cringing air." When she spoke in Columbia, South Carolina, Dickinson was happy to note that her audience included "a curious mixture of really elegant looking 'rebels'—& equally elegant looking colored people," leading her to conclude that "'Civil Rights' is an established fact in S.C." Yet, the prescient orator seemed to see the handwriting on the wall. Governor Chamberlain might be enjoying some popularity, but she worried that "the old rebels are simply using him to get such & such people & obstacles out of their way, & when they see a path clear, they will put him & his to the wall, & ride in again triumphantly." The white outcry in Charleston following her friendly chat with Robert Purvis seemed a precursor of things to come. In contrast, Dickinson concluded that white Virginians—regardless of their racial prejudices—seemed most committed to a successful interracial future. "The truth is that Virginians hate the Republic & Republican institutions far more than they could have ever hated under any condition the negroes. . . . If they can make the blacks their allies in their new crusade against Democratic institutions, I'm sure they will." As much as Dickinson detested the Virginians' love of their Confederate heroes and monuments, she seemed to conclude that the future of the South was best left to white Southerners who understood that their own self-interest lay in interracial cooperation, rather than Republican governments run by even the most politically astute carpetbaggers.

Dickinson finished her journeys with the conviction that improvements would have to come from within the South rather than be imposed by hated Northerners, with compulsory education and penal reform high on her list of suggested improvements. But although she had seen ample evidence of whites and blacks peacefully coexisting, her month in the South left her with little optimism for the immediate future. As a professional venture, the tour was a mixed success. She and Bernard had managed to cover their expenses, but she had not earned any additional money to send home to her mother. On the other hand, she did return to the North with ample fodder for future writings.

It is not clear why she never attempted to publish these letters in some form. Perhaps she thought that her jottings from her western journeys, which she published as *A Ragged Register* in 1879, were a more appropriate light fare for the reading public. On the eve of the election of 1876, she may have concluded that her readers would have little stomach for her observations on the Reconstruction South. Fortunately for us, they survive as a marvelous record of a crucial moment in our history.

Anna Dickinson's letters are housed in the Library of Congress, in the Anna Elizabeth Dickinson Papers. They are also available in twenty-five reels of microfilm. Nearly all of these four letters can be found in these papers in her Family Letters, container 3, folder 7 (microfilm reel 3). As explained in the text, a portion of the letter describing her Richmond visit has been misfiled and is at the end of her Family Letters in container 4, folder 17.

A word about editorial method: Dickinson's handwriting is sometimes difficult to decipher, although most words can be identified by considering the context. A vociferous reader and frequent author, Dickinson was a good speller with often atrocious handwriting. When she clearly misspelled a word, the error is reproduced here. But where the handwriting is too murky to distinguish each letter, no effort has been made to identify possible spelling errors. Where the level of confidence is less high, or the apparent combination of letters makes no obvious sense, the guessed word is shown in square brackets. In a few cases, an ink stain or indecipherable scribbles leave no room for educated guesses; here the omitted words are marked with "[. . .]." In a very few cases, "[*sic*]" notes an omission or error in the original.

Like many of her peers, Dickinson was more casual about punctuation than spelling. She frequently omitted closing quotation marks or periods at the end of sentences. The former have been added, marked with square brackets. Dickinson also made extremely liberal use of dashes of varying lengths, often in combination with other punctuation. These have been reproduced as em dashes.

Raleigh, North Carolina

4.10.1875

Dearest Marmee,[1] I have been so mauled about, have gazed and gawked so constantly when I have not been in the cars & have been so ready to get into bed when the time came as not to have sent any letters, tho have sent many thoughts to thee.[2]

It was a curious change—that from New York to Washington.—I put off my seal skin jacket that morning, & shivered a little in my heavy brown suit, in which I was almost cooked before I reached my journey's end.

It is a great relief that travellers have in these days in the "Washington Limited," a special express, carrying only drawing room cars & making but four or five stops & these very brief ones between N.Y. and Washington,—leaving at 9:30 A.M. & reaching its destination at[3]

I suppose the people who get from London to Liverpool would think it no great matter but it is a vast improvement on the old method of lumbering along.

Before we got to Washington I fell into the hands of the Philistine, that is to say of *a* Philistine—one of his sort would be quite enough for *any* encounter.—A tall gaunt, ungainly, slab sided fellow, with dry, coarse, unkempt hair & beard,—shiny broadcloth—greasy shiny—indifferent linens,—muddy of complexion, mean of feature, cold

& ferrety of eye, self conscious & underbred of manner planted himself in the chair beside me & presented himself as the Rev. Mr. Talmage.[4]—

I was genuinely surprised. He is a man for whom I have no admiration, seeming to me a vulgar pretentious fellow whose whole effort is to make himself conspicuous at *any* rate, but I had expected to see something marked & magnetic of appearance & manner.

He held forth about Moody and Sankey with effusiveness, & I suppose expected me to say something about *his* call to that harvest field, but as I had no opinion to express save to commiserate Brooklyn on his further stay in its midst, & to congratulate England on escaping this infliction it is as well perhaps that my opinion was kept to myself.[5]

Washington did look pleasantly when we came into it.—The swelling trees, the bits of tender green here & there on the ground, the balmy hazy air, & delicious spring atmosphere to the clouds & sky were altogether satisfactory to eyes & senses tired out by an interminable winter of cold & storms.

After I found my room at the Arlington I wandered round for an hour or so, sniffing the comforting air, & looking at the pretty little parks & at the White House grounds. *They* are pretty enough, but the house itself is certainly a disgrace to the republic. So many people, from abroad, must make a sort of estimate of us from this house in which we lodge our Chief. It is a sort of national disgrace.—nothing can be said in its behalf on the score of Republican simplicity—for look at the Capitol & the millions there spent & the yet greater millions wasted.[6] It is a mean, skimpy, [. . .]itable looking place.

No doubt good enough for the *man* who now inhabits it, but not good enough for the President of the U.S.—even tho' he be Andy Johnson, or Gen. U. S. Grant.[7]

When I came to pay my bill the next morning I fell into a fresh rage over the universal swindling of our Hotel system.—The prices are thievish to begin with, if one did but pay for what one has, but they are highway robbery on their universal plan of charging you for a multitude of things you neither have nor desire.

I got to the hotel in time to eat a five o'clock dinner if I had wanted it—which I didn't—since I had already eaten and paid for one dinner that day, with tea following, which I desired not, with supper which I both desired & devoured—with a night's lodging, & a start the next morning at 6.30,—in time to eat *some* sort of an apology for breakfast had I so minded—or stomached—neither mind nor stomach consenting.

What I had, & for what I ought to have paid was supper & lodging—$5 & dear at that.—for what I did pay was dinner, tea, supper, lodging, breakfast—& I suppose "sundries"—for the bill was $7.

Our whole hotel system ought to be over hauled and revised, & unless Americans were the most long suffering and foolishly patient of travellers, it *would* have been long since.

By night you go through to Richmond on all rail travel, by morning boat to miles & from thence by rail.[8]—The boat was nothing very fine, but comfortable with a decent breakfast, & a small army of Ethiopian servants, who claw your hand baggage & check it, & hover over it, & over you till they get you planted in the train, & stick closer than a brother to your Northern pocket book till it has opened in their behalf.[9]—Every body south of Washington—white & black—is poorer than poorly & regards a Northern person as a god send—to pick clean to the bones.

We went past that dingy, dusty shambling town of Alexandria at which I looked with sad interest remembering what brave young eyes had looked their first at it & their last at life fourteen years ago, & thought to myself—"What price was Ellsworth's young & brave, How weigh the gift that Lyon gave, Or count the cost of Winthrop grave?"[10]

We could see very little of Mount Vernon save the high river bank as we went by—but the boat's bell kept up such a melancholy tolling as to rather depress than elevate you with the thought that here had lived the "father of his country." Why they didn't give us a little life in the sound I don't know, but the bell struck solemnly, & at long intervals as tho' we were mourners at a funeral.

As I was sitting outside looking at what might possibly be seen, there came from the cabin a fat, fussy, red faced little man, & a tall scrawny woman, who, on seeing me beat a precipitate retreat. They had been in the omnibus coming from the Arlington to the boat, & proceeded to announce, the one to the other—

He, "Mr. Longfellow arrived last night,—I am so sorry we had to leave before seeing him,—" Magnificent glance around at the small fry seated about him.

She,—"Sis & I hear Miss Dickinson came in. Sent to her room but she had retired.—So sorry,—been such a great while since I had a good long talk with her."—Compound magnificent glance around,—small fry one & all silent & admiring.

I suppose they had been going through an enlightening process, for when they next saw *one* of the small fry they [. . .] retreated.

Just out of Fredericksburg we passed one of the National Cemeteries,—There are four grades or classes (according to number of internments) this is one of the first class,—lying on the side of a high hill, beautifully terraced the little mounds one & all green with growing spring, & their white head boards showing plain in the soft verdure, the flag, for which the men under it had died, flying from a mound at the top.—15[,]241 of these dead heroes, but 2397 of them known, 12,844, with no name on their head stones save "Unknown Soldier of the U.S."

They are men who fell at Fredericksburg & in the Wilderness, but chiefly on that most disastrous of days at Chancellorsville.[11]

Virginia looks very little richer than when we saw it ten years ago. The train was an improvement on the cattle bodies we then inhabited, but the country has the same *open* & dreary look,—the fences still down, the fields largely uncultivated—a scrubbly growth of trees taking the place of the stumps of forests we there saw.—The towns are dusty & frowsy, & the people, black & white, dustier & frowsier.

We got into Richmond about one o'clock to find a wretched *pen*—of a depot—the most of it *out doors,* crowded, with a miscellaneous faire of dirty & idle people,—& for my part, I fell into a struggle with Miss Van Lew about the custody of my own person,—she being determined to take me to her home, & I being equally determined to find myself at a hotel,—finally we compromised, Bernard retired to the St James with my baggage, & I went home with her to dinner.[12]

She it was who did such noble service for our soldiers during the war.—She & all her family.—an old Virginia family it is, once rich & with plenty of slaves, but ardent Unionists.—How many of the family may still exist I know not, but that at the old homestead consists of Miss Van Lew, her mother, her brother, & his two daughters—old Mrs. Van Lew is a real lady of the by-gone time, small & slight & half blind, but full of deep feeling & intelligence.[13] The brother is well informed, but with the shambling manner & lazy tho' inflated style of speech that is universal here—but a good fellow,—the daughters are a jolly, warm hearted couple of girls,—as for Miss Van Lew, she is a curiosity,—a little *wizened* woman, skinny and parched, with a frowzle of curls, thin face, clear blue eyes, little claws of hands, & the most intense, nervous organization & manner I ever saw.—I wonder she had succeeded in keeping out of an insane asylum.—I suppose she was high strung to begin with & the unceasing agony she endured on account of our prisoners has nearly made a wreck of her.

She isn't a bit like a northern strong minded woman.—Romantic & a bit sentimental, in spite of her being such an absolute old maid. Bored of finery tho' with the universal, bad southern taste in getting it and putting it on.—Fond of novels & poetry, & quotations, yet with a record that would put even brave men to the blush, & doing work, at present, that very few men could perform half so well.

She went into the prisons & took help to our men when it was taking her own life in her hands.—smuggled things & money to them, smuggled letters away from them, spent her own money, sold her land, got into debt to raise means to help their necessities,—placed in danger of death again and again by helping men to escape, & actually concealing them in her house, where they were disguised & from whence they went homeward rejoicing.

Six years ago she was appointed Post Mistress here, & has made an excellent one.—I went into the post-office & found nearly all of the clerks & attendants colored men. With two or three original union men, who were white, one of them a great brawny Irishman.—But as Miss Van Lew said "the most faithful creatures alive,"—& with one shrewd, wide awake Yankee girl from Maine who has been head clerk here for some years. She has been in Va for nine years, but part of that time as teacher of a freedman's school.

Miss Van evidently believes in *representing* all classes of the people.

She is almost adored by the colored people whose friend she has always been. Nearly all of her old slaves are about her. Some in her house, some employed at the post office. One of these, she says, the best man in the place.—She has spoken to them at various times, & has prevented trouble again and again.—But she is frightfully unpopular with the whites, even with the Union people.—It is quite natural that when she feels so deeply and has suffered so much she should be an extremist.—A black is evidently not only as good as a white to her, but a good bit better.—She treats her servants & employees as she never would think of doing if they were whites, & she has absolutely no toleration for those who may be quite as earnest as she, tho' not in her way.

She regarded me as next to a demi-god before I came & for that matter till after I had been so praised by the Richmond papers, when she began to look at me suspiciously,—but when the *Dispatch* announced—tho' with no more show of authority from me than from her that I was opposed to the Civil Rights Bill, she came to see me and nearly picked my eyes out.

However she was & is too good a soul to fall out with, & I took her in hand & gave her such a talking to, as make her fall to weeping, & at last she took me into her little sticks of arms, & into her favor once more.

As to the Civil Rights Bill, I never *was* in favor of it, & my look at things hereabouts has not changed my opinion.[14]—It has been a bit of political wire pulling—with the exception of Mr. Sumner's work—from beginning to end.[15]—The colored people don't want it, & it has only stirred up fresh antagonism against them on the part of the whites.—I have spoken to every darkey with whom

I have come in contact about it, & they are all of one mind,—they either care nothing about it or they want none of it.

I was amused at our head waiter at the St. James,—Charlie,—a very intelligent fellow who had belonged to one of the "very first families in Virginia."—& who had been North, as body servant since the war.—'Go inside dat theatre' said he. "We. De colored people have got dere own churches & dere own societies, & dere own associations & amusements, & dey have companies of dere own. Dey don't go where they are not wanted, & dey don't want to go.—now dere is dat theatre.—De proprietor is a *lady*!!—Why I wouldn't wait on her in dis room. & de white folks what crowd into de place, wouldn't sit *here* at de same table with her. *Dey* may do it, but I likes to preserve de harmonious,—I wouldn't go into *her* house any more than de proprietors would have her come in here.["]—& Charlie was done—the poor woman, be it known, is of very questionable, or rather unquestionable reputation.

The St. James, to which I went is a very neat, comfortable little hotel.—The Exchange is larger, & quite as good, but not so quiet.—The dirty, old Spotswood was burned down about five years ago.—fortunately—for nothing short of fire would have ever cleaned it of the vermin I am sure.—The cooking was fair, tho' nothing to boast of (& getting worse every day since we left Richmond.)

All the burned district is rebuilt, & in very fair shape.—far better than any of the old business places that were left standing.—A few of the buildings are really fine tho' none of them are remarkable & you smile as you hear these people say, in perfect good faith, that they have the finest city, & the best business quarters in the country.—one of the editors took me to the exchange,—where were about a dozen or so of tobacco factors, & about as much stir as you would say in some up street in New York when business was slack,—& asked me if that did not rival the famous NY stock exchange—whereat I smiled softly.

The ignorance,—the ignorance native, & the ignorance of non-acquisition, the pomp, the vanity, the bombast, the spoiled-child [. . .], & bad temper of these people is simply incredible if you did not see it.

They know nothing,—they have been no where, they are surrounded by the civilization of a century ago, they are poverty stricken in ability, money, & personal resources,—they are ill informed as to all other parts of the world, & the every day life outside. They have the manners of proud backwoodsmen & they *really* & *honestly* believe there is no such place & there are no such people under the sun as this state of Virginia & they its sons & daughters.—They are worse than an [. . .], if you could not afford to laugh at them—which save you from sickness.

The tobacco [trade] is a very heavy one, & some of the factors had proceeded to cut off their noses to spite their faces by closing the factories. Everything here is dull enough when these are running, & with these idle the place is as cheerful as a cemetery.

The streets, as thee must remember, are wide, but they are broken & shockingly paved, both in the center & the side walks, dust in heaps, & a plenty of broken stones.—Insufficiently lighted at night & ill cared for by day or by night.

Even the new and really handsome main business street has a dreary & *un* business like air,—the shop keepers loll over their counters & stand at the doors,—& off this street one wonders how the shop keepers live at all.[16]

Every where are swarms & swarms of colored people their hands in their pockets, their backs against the wall, talking or blinking in the sun, & yet the colored people are the only ones who seem to have any thing *to do.* They are the servants, & the drivers, & half the small shop, & stall keepers, & the laboring people generally—so imagine the idle whites,—tho' the most of those do not lounge quite so openly as the idle blacks.

There is one comfort tho' for the city, everybody is poor, & everybody knows that everybody is poor, & nobody pretends to be anything else. The "*first* families," go about in ill fitting boots, & battered hats, & limp linens & shabby looking, badly made clothes,—& the working people & the poor people live & array themselves with seeming comfort in a fashion what would make a good many Northern paupers rise in rebellion.[17]

It was a mystery to me how the most of the people lived at all, for there really did not seem enough money in circulation to keep a mouse alive.—When the factories begin work again I suppose things will be somewhat better.—Still the colored people manage to get along better than their poor white confederates,—& they all help one another.—There is a wonderful unity among them for help & brotherhood,—& on Sunday, at the African Church they made as tidy & even fine a show as tho' they had been people very well to do in this world's ways.

The State House grounds looked quite handsomely, save for the blemish of the statue of Washington, & the convicts who were lounging about.

The Washington Monument, in all save the statue, is no mean matter.—There is a solid & well proportioned base surmounting which & girdling the shaft are a row of standing & a row of sitting figures.—The standing figures being portrait statues & the sitting figures allegorical & emblematical.

Marshall—the sitting figure in front representing *Justice.*

Nelson—Finance
Jefferson—Independence
Mason—Bill of Rights
P Henry—Revolution
Lewis—Colonial Times

—But the Cap Stone is an equestrian statue of Washington that is fearful & wonderful to behold—no horse could hold that position for thirty seconds, & the face & figure of his rider rival one another in want of beauty, elegance & expression.—The face looks towards the State house & the hand points towards a certain other prominent public building.—Gov. Wise, who whatever his political sins, had admirable taste, & was duly disgusted with the monument, was once asked the meaning of the attitude, & answered it was the one good thing about the monstrosity, it looked at the members of the legislature where they *were,* & pointed warningly—or suggestively to the place where they *ought* to be—the Penitentiary,—which would apply to some other capitals than Richmond.[18]

This interesting legislature (not the one Wise criticized) adjourned the evening I got to Richmond & regaled itself with secession speeches a plenty.—Its chief work was a series of laudations of Gen. Lee—That he was the greatest wisest, best, most humane, most christian like soldier & statesman the world had *ever* seen.—That if *he* had been left to his own devices, unmolested by lesser men (that was a jab at Jeff Davis) the war would have had a very different ending.—I doubt whether in the hottest days of the war wilder eulogies of Lee & more hot bitterness towards his opponents was ever displayed.—The six or seven colored members of this legislature must have had a good time of it.—They sat in one corner, to themselves, & were plentifully black guarded, but had their revenge whenever a bill was pending that needed their votes, by seeing these bitter enemies of theirs run to, & button hole, & entreat of them as tho' they had been "men & bretheren."

I noticed the next morning's papers were careful to have no report of their seditious speeches—The papers *might* be read by *Northern* eyes else where, & commented on!

These papers, & the leaders of opinion here are wonderfully cautious & prudent.—Wonderfully so.—They have the name in this section, (amongst *us,*) of being fiery quick, imprudent.—They are shrewder than the shrewdist Yankees.—Body & soul, root & branch, through & through they *hate! hate! hate!* us.—Every body who comes in contact with them feels it not because they want us to but because, in spite of themselves their very atmosphere betrays it, but they constantly [. . .] & preach & exercise prudence of writing, & speech & action till the brightening future dawns.

—Woe betide this Republic if *that* day ever breaks on it.

Of course thee remembers the state house itself, with the quaint old statue of Washington,—its quaint old bust of Lafayette, both voted and paid for first after the Revolutionary days, its four story stove 150 years old, that at one time was the only means of heating the whole building.—

The Senate Chamber & Hall of Delegates are a good deal cleaner & neater than when we saw them before.—Tidy carpets on the floors, desks & chairs, not fine but substantial & well looking.—On the walls of the Hall of Delegates a portrait of Chatham in ridiculous Roman toga & bare legs, on one side the door,—a full length of Jefferson on the other. Going into the Senate Chamber I looked for the picture *there,* & found nothing but a bare new, brilliantly tinted, elaborately framed portrait of Robert E. Lee in the post of honor.

Up in the Library are a many memorials of old Colonial & Revolutionary days, & portraits of all the old Virginia governors & worthies, hung high on the walls, while lower down, on every available space are suspended Johnson (Joe E) & Stonewall Jackson, & the leaders Civil & Military of the Rebellion, with Lee, Lee, Lee in every shape & form.—It is reasonable to say that in the estimation of multitudes here, this speaker of solemn oaths, this renegade to his flag, this false soldier, this traitorous citizen, this butcher & murderer, under whose command were enacted the horrors of Libby Prison & Belle Isle,—is absolutely above God Almighty, & in the estimation of the rest of them, second to Him alone.[19]

On the table, in the middle of the room is Valentine's bust known as "The Nation's Ward" a grinning darkey, with ragged shirt, canteen slung over his shoulders a battered, torn U.S. soldier cap on his head, & the head that of an Idiot.[20]

All about the building cleaning it, as all about the grounds putting them in order were numbers of colored convicts, in their striped prison dress, with their armed guards watching them.—a degrading sight.

I did mean to go to the prison, but even Miss Van Lew dissuaded me.—She told me, from immediate observation that it was so horribly filthy & so swarming with vermin, as to make it an absolutely dangerous place for a visitor to enter.

Thee remembers the Jeff Davis head quarters, of course. The big, roomy handsome house, with the pretty garden the big, pillared back portico looked out upon?—Well it is used now for a negro school.—Where once was the head & front of the effort to reduce these people to a hopeless beastiality, is how a school to elevate them to a *real* humanity.—The mills of the gods grind slowly but[21]—

The markets are shabby, close, ill smelling & dirty, &

pretty much all the old picturesque effect of darkey "outstanders" is gone.

Libby Prison & Castle Thunder have been resolved into their original conditions of Tobacco Warehouses.—I walked round & round them, but would not go in,—they made me sick only to look at them,—at the agony, & heroism & martyrdom, these [senseless] walls have looked upon!—I wonder they did not fall.—I wonder that the men who owned them did not tear down the proof of the awful cruelty they & theirs had here seen inflicted & been responsible for the inflicting.—I wonder what stolidity, what brutishness can possess these people, that they deliberately paint a sign board—Libby Prison & put it out for travellers as tho' it were a wonder, or beauty of the place, to which they are ready or proud to call attention.[22]

I went out to Hollywood, which looked very much as it did ten years ago.—Over on the hill side are the six or seven thousand rebel soldiers lying—with little pegs driven in as head stones, with bits of zinc with name, regiment & date nailed to these.—Not pretty to look at, but I suppose enduring.—But the graves of the two generals who here lie Stuart & Hill, are just as we saw them, without monument or stone. Stuart with a little wooden head board, but Hill with nothing at all to mark his grave.[23]

There is a "soldiers monument" that is a spectacle to behold.—A *pyramid* of broken granite stone, solidly built, & about 180 ft high—I should say as a guess.—as rough, ugly & ungainly as tho' it were the work of the Druids, or were a Scottish [cairn] of a thousand years ago.—No symmetry, no poetry,—nothing noble, nothing ideal, nothing either noble or suggestive,—a work of barbarians. The intention has been, I believe, to have ivy grown over it, but no ivy grows.[24]

$17,000 were raised to build this monstrosity.—It never cost a third of that sum,—some rebel contractor has amused himself, as contractors elsewhere have done by growing rich on the spoils of the credulous.—If you ask these people *why* the thing is what it is, they tell you, as they are constantly telling you that they are too poor to have anything better.—That is a note they are *never* tired of playing upon, their over [. . .], their universal poverty—for which *they* are responsible?—Oh no.—In which we of the North are responsible. *They* desired no war.—We have stripped, robbed, destroyed them.

However they are rich enough to have spent I dont know how many thousands of dollars to have a full length reclining figure of Lee, put into marble for the Lexington College of which he was President. Valentine,—their one artist here, is responsible for it & was anxious to have me see it.—Mr. James, the City Editor of the Enquirer came to wait upon me to the studio.—one of the very first of the F.F.V.'s—a youth who informed me that he had never done anything before the war, & had never expected to do anything, but who *had* to support himself, & found no pleasure, but only an intolerable weariness in the doing,—who informed me further that Equality & its proclamation, Republicanism, or rather Democracy & its workings were stupendous lies & humbugs.—That there *was* an aristocracy, & the only true aristocracy of *birth* & *blood,* & that in its perfection, in this land it could only be found in Virginia—he being one of the representatives!

A [slimfry], inelegant figure, with an indifferent head, low, flat forhead & weak, pretty features, a quantity of lank, light hair, sparse light moustache, pasty white skin with the blotches on it, & the crumbling teeth marking exceeding poverty of blood, & want of vitality.

An aristocrat—quotha!

Apparently they have but one studio at Richmond for

when we got into the carriage James said—"to the studio"—& to the studio of Valentine we went.

A large & rather pleasant room, with the statue on a raised platform in the centre of it,—& a very beautiful work of art it is.—The figure is a little above life size, recumbent, but with the head & chest raised as they might be by a cushion. The head lies to the right, slightly, the right hand on the chest, the left fallen easily & at full length with the hand resting open on a sword, the feet are crossed & over all is thrown a bit of drapery like a cloak.—The idea is of rest after warfare, & is beautifully executed,—the whole effect one of nobility & repose. The execution is very elaborate & fine, & the marble an exceptionally fine piece.[25]

A procession of people was moving through during the half hour I remained—"The best people" in the city, & never saw I more grief, admiration, love & reverence displayed.

Some "ladies" who were there desired to be presented to me, & were presented. Very pretty, very soft & sweet spoken,—who, shortly after the introduction proceeded to call my attention to two "groups" standing in a corner near.—The one "The Nation's Ward" before described,—the other "Knowledge is Power."—A negro boy, dirty, ragged, forlorn, with great, splay fat & clumsy head fallen to one side, mouth gaping & eyes closed in sound sleep, with an open book lying on his knee.

The attention was called as tho' they were doing the most gracious of deeds,—"I thought you would like to see this" said one. "I appreciate the kindness madame" said I, bland & smiling as she.

What occupation for a man of real genius, to use that genius for the purpose of ridiculing & degrading those who are poor, friendless, & struggling against a thousand odds & difficulties!

Valentine himself later in calling my attention to the busts, & to *every* thing else in fact in the room passed these in silence. Here as everywhere in the south it is the women & the clergymen who hold fast to their meanness & hate.

Tho' I was amused at my "aristocratic" companion. If he had known anything of the ordinary usage of polite society he would know that it is the *invariable* rule for a lady or gentleman,—where there is only a coachman,—to open the carriage door—a sure sign of country or parvenu training to wait for the man to clamber from his box to open for the insiders. When we got to the studio James waited till it was so foolish & awkward I opened the door myself, when of course he sprang out, saying "of course *he* couldn't get down"—& mumbling to himself in a breath "the damned nigger," tho' he had just before been telling me how much he liked the colored people, & what good terms the two races, here, were on.

It is true that the Virginians do like the blacks, & treat them far better than the people in some other sections.—The servants were very largely house servants, the most of them *children* of the house, of superior intelligence, proud of the family to which they belonged, subjected to no outrage since the war.—Also the people here have had the good sense to see that the best thing for all concerned was to have good schools for those who are to vote, & the schools are admirable & abundant. So far as I could see (admirable for this section.)

The truth is that Virginians hate the Republic & Republican institutions far more than they could have ever hated under any condition the negroes. They love State Sovereignty far better than they ever loved slavery, & if they can make the blacks their allies in their new crusade against Democratic institutions, I'm sure they will,—& to that end are they working.

Who should appear on the field of action on Sunday morning but Julia Gould![26] Looking well, & behaving very sensibly. She had been for two months in the South visiting schools—colored schools.—She asked for "Mother & Susan" with a great show of affection & desired her love sent to them.

I went in the afternoon to our National Cemetery near Richmond.[27]—There is a lodge, & the usual mound with the flagstaff, & the regulation monument an upright cannon with a little pyramid of cannon balls planted at the four corners of the space about it,—& the long, long rows of white head stones, at the ends of the long, long rows of little green graves.—Some of them having names—a few,—the great body of them with one

Unknown Soldier
of
the U.S.

or with two, or three sometimes marked in the grave. —Many of these men who perished in the long agony of Libby Prison or the slow torture of Belle Isle.

On the cannon is a shield, the shield telling how this Cemetery was established in Sep. 1866,—and how here there lie 6529 men.—838 of them known, *5691 unknown.*

"*Thou* knowist" I thought as I looked with dim eyes.

The cemetery has the regulation stone wall about it, & at the corners of the drive there are some patriotic verses painted on a species of sign boards, but no landscape gardening has here been done, & the place has an angular & military look very different from that at Raleigh.

Sunday evening I went to the African Church,—where the blacks were so long preached to by their white masters,—no negro being allowed in the pulpit,—& where the "Southern heart" was again and again "fired anew." The blacks are so foolish as to have determined to tear it down and build another & larger one in its stead.

It is only the "low down niggers" here who are Methodists,—the "quality" are Baptist.—All desire to belong to the "quality,"—the result is that this church which can seat about 3000 has a membership of almost six thousand.—Instead of dividing,—or building a great addition to this building,—or putting up an entirely new one elsewhere,—they know so little as to drag down this place that would be regarded, in the future, as the spot of most real historic interest in all Richmond, putting out of sight those at which I had looked in the morning.—The old, old frame one in which Patrick Henry had "fired the hearts" of other men in a past time for freedom. The Memorial Church, built on the site of the burned theatre with the names of those who had suffered carved on the monument in the quaint open space of the church's portico, & the Episcopal Church in which Robert Lee "worshipped"—& where he was worshipping on that eventful 2 of April when the telegram was brought him, that his lines were cut through, & that he could no longer defend Richmond.—That must have been a tremendous day when these people learned that the backbone of their Rebellion was *indeed broken*.[28]

—I did mean to tell thee of the sermon & services,—but wandered off after other matters.—One hears very little of Congregational singing now amongst these people—more's the pity.—They must be like "white folks."—& so wherever they can scare up a melodeon they proceed to play away on it, & to have a dozen or so of singers in the choir "[wrastle]" with regulation hymns & anthems,—to the misery of all cultivated ears, while they sit still in admiring silence.

We had been misinformed as to the time of service,

& so got a little of the old fashioned melody.—half-past-seven *we* thought was the time that proved to be eight,—& we were told we must go early as there was always a great crowd.—Long before even half past seven the place was full, & some brother struck up a hymn, the others joining in.—Still it was only a *regulation* hymn.—By & by an old darkey who sat on the pulpit stairs began one of the plantation wails,—a few joined in, but one of the numerous preachers sitting near checked him with the request that "something should be sung that they could all join in."—& so another hymn was begun.—The fact being, of course that every mother's son & daughter of them knew the first far better than the last, but as we afterwards discovered from the people sitting about us, "dey do *dis*-courage de singing of such now."—specially, I think, when there are quite a number of "de white folks" present.

However, the old fellow was not to be snubbed & the hymn being through he began again, on another outbreak.—*That* was too much for them. Presently there was a sort of *boom* through the house—like the far off sound of the sea, from mouths & feet, & hands on knees, that gradually took the distinct melody, & at last they joined in.—It seemed to be about "Jesus" & "de cross" & "fight on ole soldiers" "fight on ole warriors"—& a refrain that was simply "ah—ah—ah—" in rising scales that was the most indescribably pathetic thing I ever heard.

The preacher was a man who has been North for a good many years, who gave us an unedifying & stupidly commonplace discourse,—making a laborious struggle after large sounding words & generally getting correct ones,—with very little of the negro dialect.—His text was "& the spirit & the bride say come"—& the only absurd announcement in connection with it was,—that "the invitashun was a sort of duo,—a duo—what might be better phrased as a [duett]—yes it was a [duett] of an invi *ta*-shun." The prolongation of the "*ta*-shun" sounding as here written was very pleasing, & I noticed it in the pronunciation of of [*sic*] kindred words, not only as he used them, but as do all the reasonably well educated Africans. The prolongation of the vowel sounds would certainly make our harsh English very much more musical.

But when he, & his chocolate colored face, & immaculate linen, & shining & elegant broad cloth had disappeared, one of the *black[est]* prayed. "He were from Georgy" my neighbors informed me,—black as coal,—a great powerful fellow with a voice like an organ, as full & as rich, & he prayed like a *battery*. The other fellow had been full of airs & graces, looking at his hands & studying his attitudes, & having very little heart or soul in him,—but this fellow was in dead earnest, & his force & fervor were enough to thrill any body.

He really meant what he said,—but what impresses me more & more is the utter absence not only of any deep feeling, but almost of any tender & earnest feeling among them.[29]

The papers at first were inclined to be very cold to me, but they after wards praise me to the skies, & the people who were literally the cream of the place, & a beautiful audience to talk to, were fairly crazy over Jean d'Arc—only there were none of them.[30]—My first audience did not pay expenses, & the second barely covered its bills

They are poor, that is one thing. The great body of the people neither know nor care anything about lectures,—that is another thing:—the women hate me & wont come to hear me,—most important thing of all!

My first audience had not a dozen women in it, & the second was not much in that respect.

Monday afternoon I came to Petersburg,—a clean

car, & good road, with an hour's run.—Directly I came in I scrambled into a carriage & went my way through the town & out towards our old camping ground.

The town really looks quite prosperous—for a Southern place. Dirty & dusty, & frowsy, with broken sidewalks & streets, but far cleaner & brighter & busier looking than Richmond.—Some new shops & handsome warehouse, & a good many really elegant new residences—conspicuous among these that of Gen. Mahone, (of the Mine fame) very large, & very expensive, but of the most remarkable hue between blue & lavender & simply hideous.[31]—The old houses, double & huge, with centre hall, plenty of trees & flowers, & lovely grounds about them abound. Petersburg, I believe, had the honor of being the most beautiful place in Va. before the war & I can readily believe it.

The tobacco factories are in full blast, so the negroes are employed, & there is money in circulation.

Driving out of the town I passed the Post Office which is new & quite handsome,—an old Masonic Hall, of antique looking bricks, with quaint looking doorways & windows, & green emblems & signs all over the face & in great staring figures 1757 (I believe tho' my memory is a little treacherous)—also then went by me a procession of colored men on foot, followed by a half-dozen carriages with some good looking colored girls rigged up in gauze & crepe headdresses & wrappings,—the men wearing some sort of green regalia over their citizens dress—a very good band of music preceding them. All of them well dressed & orderly,—the whole thing very like an ordinary turnout of temperance, or Masonic or odd fellow organizations elsewhere,—but thee can see what the Petersburg paper finds in it,—a return to baffoonery. Thee can see its comments for thyself.[32]

Of course I went to the old church at Blanford built

in 1735,—now a ruin, but in excellent preservation, the walls thick & strong, & the whole place made most beautiful by the dense masses of ivy growing over it,—dense & green all the year round.[33] Did we, or did we not go to it when we were before here?—The walls are here & there pierced with shot, & there are some gaps in the walls made by shell—& up at the altar end, on the walls is a tablet with the names of the *old* men, the "first citizens of the place" who were called upon by the last requisition of the Rebel government, & "served their country" till, I believe, they died.

All about in the old, old country are marks of a conflict strangely at variance with this stillness, & many & many an old wall & tomb have been shattered by what was intended to bring death to the living, & not spend forces uselessly on the dead.

It is a beautiful place spite of its not being well kept.—lovely old trees,—endless masses of sweet scented flowers,—high grass crowded now with wild violets,—stones & memorials beautiful with the beauty of age, mellowed & grey & brown.—The people of a past time were determined their dead should not escape from their abiding places for their lots instead of being simply marked off,—or surrounded by a light iron railing were compassed about by many brick walls.

Some of the Rebel dead are buried here—& I noticed arches put up over them on one of which is marked "Our Dead"—on another "Tried & True" on the one side, on the other "Our Noble Defenders" & flowers growing & cut were all over their graves.—A little distance from these stands a shaft to the memory of the soldiers of a past war.—"A Tribute to Patriotism" as it bears on its face to men who died for fame & freedom." Curious contradictions, these, of faith & sentiment.—Gen. Mahone has a brand new tomb, as ugly & pretentious as his brand new house,—a big temple of a place, & of a slate blue color, standing off in the solitude & of a hill side where some Confederate soldiers are buried.

Mahone is the General for whom Fort Damnation is named.[34]—(That is to say Fort Hell & Fort Damnation are really Fort Mahone & Fort Sedgwick)—& thee must remember them,—they are the two forts that have but the width of the country road between them, & where the firing was so hot & awful.—They are the only forts now standing save Fort Steadman, & they are greatly worn down. Mahone is now the president of a rail road with a salary of $18000 a year.—I saw him while at P.—a medium height,—*very* slender, with thin, gaunt face & long lank hair, & a very hard stern expression on his thin features. He it was who was so ferocious at the "mine"—giving orders for "no quarter" to the colored soldiers.[35]

Right opposite the cemetery is a new colored cemetery.—Why they should want to get so near the white people, dead, who hated & wronged them so living, is one of the problems.

Farther on is a Jewish cemetery.

Mainly all the fortifications have disappeared.—Ploughed down & planted over, largely by tobacco. The crater has been dug over & over for relics, the earth has sunken down, & been flung up till very little of the original shape remains, & not half the sign.—One can yet see the mouth where the explosion broke out,—& one can trace the line of the mine straight away from the "Crater" for the eighth, or the greater of a mile to the line of timber where the men began operations.—My colored driver was in the town that day, & came out when the awful din of the explosion was heard.—The rebels were of course driven out of the exploded fort, & a little way back towards the town but rallied behind some temporary earthworks & fought till they drove back our troops, & recovered their lost ground.—The fighting between this temporary line of defense & the Crater must have been awful.—"De flame of de guns, & de flames of de drums sounded *all* de time—& was just awful. You couldn't hear yourself hollow."—said my African.—& "When some of us came out to bury de dead dey was so thick across dere—waving his hand over the contested space. "We couldn't step widout treading on dem."

Now all that terrible field has been ploughed over & marked down in tobacco.

Somebody lives here, & they have built a little house, & have relics for sale in it, right by the mine.—They looked to me very tame——& somewhat *suspicious,* remembering the time that had elapsed since '65 & the probable number of relic seekers.—Some, I mean, when I thought of the scene when we beheld it, & of the fragments of dead men who were buried under us.—Never shall I forget the sick feeling that went all over me when I, dragging at a bayonet that came very slowly to the surface dragged out with it the blue coated arm of a black soldier,—& I think, John—was it—found a hand somewhere when he stooped for a relic.[36]

Fort Steadman was so much more securely built than the others, with solid timber under the earth works, as to have resisted wind & weather—tho' it has very much changed in form,—& the [garrisons] are all gone, of course, long ago burned for fire wood. In the fort one or two cabins are standing inhabited by some darkies.

What hot work has been been [*sic*] done here!—The rebel line of works was but 600 ft away, & the picket lines but 200 ft apart.

The gully into which I plunged for a walk, & where the dead lying in the high grass, is nearly gone,—the change of water course has filled it, & washed it away at the sides to almost a level.

I lived over again that blazing day, & its sad & terrible scenes, with a distinctness that made it seem like a yesterday.

The house was slim,—of course,—tho' here, as at Richmond I had a picked audience, & I will say this for all of my Va audiences that while they were small in size,—in point of enthusiasm, friendliness, quick apprehension, keen sympathy, & magnetic helpfulness I never saw them surpassed.[37]—As for the North Carolina ones they are dumb as dogs.—The next morning I went over the largest tobacco factory & through a white & colored public school—& was interested in both,—but I believe more in the first—that is to say the factory, than in the second.

The factory is simply a huge warehouse,—with the leaves tied up in bunches, as it is picked & sent in, on the *first* floor,—here were men & women, or rather boys & women picking them apart, & sorting them out flat to be carried to a huge vat in which they are steeped in a compound of licorice & gum-arabic water—which water also holds divine sweet tasting & spicy things.—from here it goes up stairs & the long stem that runs up the middle of the leaf is picked out, & the leaves are rolled into "quids," some in an oblong shape, soft & smooth, & some twisted.—It is curious to watch the men working on these.—Some of them work so fast, taking the short leaves for the inside the long ones for the outside—to make a fair show—as to be almost magical.—Knowing both weight and size by *instinct,* or rather by constant practice & habit,—for they do not even look at the scales that hang by them,—&, as the freemen told me, out of thousands, there would not be the variation of pins weight.—I suppose a good *substantial* pin!

The superintendent of public instruction was with me, & the owner of the factory with his brother-in-law.—All of them red-head fire eaters,—yet they had to confess, when I asked them that the system of free labor was paying them a great deal better than the old slave labor ever had done. Tho' I noticed a satirical smile on Mr. Leavenworth's face when I said "I presume this sort of labor pays better than the *old* style" & he answered in what was expected evidently to convey a denial to me—"do you *think* so?"—To which I was expected to make no answer I suppose,—but having made answer—"Yes I *do* think so.—am I wrong?"—His smile vanished, & a frown took its place but he answered, "No, you are right,"—"but," as one of the others added "the negroes are hopelessly lazy,—they don't like to work, & the deteriorating effect of the change of condition will be marked on them in the next generation."—All the same I notice they are the only people here abouts who *do* the work, whether they like it or not.

And yet, in a sense, they are right in their assertions,—the negroes of the growing generation unless something is soon done for them in the way of compulsory education & training schools for work, will sink far below the old slaves.—*They* felt the need of education & were eager to learn,—also, they had *trained* habits of industry,—& after their fling for a little while, through which they thought freedom did mean the taking possession of all their masters had,—& doing nothing,—they settled—in almost all cases, to steady work,—or some sort of work in nearly all cases.—But the little darkeys have no one to control them,—no one to make them work, & their fathers & mothers in a great many cases are more anxious,—like almost all very poor people,—to have their children assist them in earning a living than in going to school,—& they are as a rule, the most idle, thieving, lying, scampish young monkeys that can be imagined.—Some effort ought to be made & be made speedily looking towards an improvement in this matter.

Virginia, without a carpet bag rule,—& with the enormous debt of $40,000,000, has nonetheless had the sense to spend as much money & effort in behalf of the colored schools as of the white.[38]—Excellent schools, with white, *home* teachers,—who understand the negroes better than Northern women can, & who evidently know how to get along with them. The Virginians have held, & are going to hold far greater influence with the colored people, than they do elsewhere in the South, just on account of this,—& otherwise they show their proverbial long headedness.—They bind the colored people to them by gratitude.—They have these colored people taught by their own old masters & mistresses—or by the children of these, & so keep the *habit* & the show of superiority & authority,—they make them reasonably well informed, industrious, & so have an immense lever to use against real Republican institutions, & *for* states rights, in some shape, in time to come.

The schools at Petersburg, for both white & colored, I found large, well ventilated, admirably arranged.—With a great many red headed, & rather slovenly young ladies, as teachers,—the daughters of men who have been very rich,—old slave holders & secessionists.—Slow as to manner, drawling as to speech, & yet, one could see with real grit in them & knowing precisely how to get along with the sort of elements with which they have to deal.

I got back in time to eat my dinner, & a capital one, at *our* old hotel.—It is now called the *City Hotel,*—and has been very much altered & furnished up.—Still it is *Southern* & no mistake,—there was a huge "side board" arrangement in my room in the shape of two stationary wash stands running across almost from wall to wall, & there was such a musty smell to the under part of it, & such a smell of dirt, & dead rot as to make me shut the doors in haste.

"Our" old mammy I saw not, but I had the same delicious corn waffles,—or their first cousins,—that we found so edible years ago,—&, to tell the truth they are the only decent specimens of corn bread I have "struck" anywhere.

Getting on to the train for Norfolk I had a bit of experience. I noticed first what I have noticed everywhere so far the unusual cleanliness of the cars.—The roads are horrible,—rough & shambling,—& the cars are apparently our refuse Northern cars, but the rear car is almost always scrupulously clean.—There is the regular smoking car forward, & there is on almost all the trains a notable "second class" coach,—a rough thing,—a cut between a very common ordinary car, & a caboose, & into this the dirty & nasty people chamber to the great relief of all decent travellers. Those who get into the other car or cars have the politeness as a rule, *not* to spit on the floor, & not to throw about a menagerie of orange & apple skins, & pea nut shells.—Still, one reason of the commended cleanliness may be the exceeding few people who travel this way, there are not enough of them to make a *very* bad dirt.

There sat in front of me a lady,—evidently a lady of her Southern kind,—middle-aged,—her husband, a fine looking man for a southerner—(they all look as tho' the effort of their lives was to prop themselves up with their hands braced in the bottom of their pockets, & their shoulders against their ears,—shambling, loose jointed, & without a spine) was smoking on the platform outside.—She leaned forward & called "George, George,—has Miss Dickinson come down yet?"—He made some pantomime which I understood, but *she* did not, & so she recommenced her inquiries,—& at last was made to understand by more pantomime & divers lip signs that Miss Dickinson had not only "come down" but was directly behind her.—She whirled round as if she had been shot, & *stared* & *stared,* & *stared* at me, till it really seemed as tho' her eyes would start from their sockets,—then abruptly turned away, & as abruptly turned back & recommenced her glaring.—Never saw I such genuine *astonishment* depicted in a face.—At least she seemed to realize *what* she was doing, & faced about once more, but, evidently, very uneasy, she turned back at last, & said "Is this Miss Anna Dickinson?" "It is" I answered. "I beg your pardon," then said she "for staring at you so—but I never was more astonished in my life.—I thought you were coming from Richmond & was asking my husband whether you really *had* come down on the train,—are you *sure* you are Miss Dickinson?"[39]

"Quite sure" said I. "Well!" she went on.—["]I *am* amazed.—I thought—why! You are the *daughter* of the Miss Dickinson I expected to see,—& you *don't* wear bloomers![40]—& you are a *lady!*["] (She didn't seem to consider what I might be making out of *her* by this performance)—"a charming young lady," & then she fell to asking me a procession of questions about my travels & about the South & what I had seen of it.—By & by her husband came in, & there was more talk. They were evidently sensible people about most matters that are here at issue.—Spoke well of the negroes,—& of the need of educating them, & of the better state of feeling that existed between them & the whites in Va, owing to the fact that almost all of them "*here*" were house servants, & so a habit of association & affection formed.—Whereas to the South, where the great plantations are, "the negroes had to live with the overseers who were very often cruel,—oh, of course,—there is no doubt of that,—*very* cruel,—& the masters & people were very wide apart, & stay so now.—A Virginia nigger["] (negro had been used consciously,—the vernacular slipped out unconsciously) "was approved of the family to which he belonged as the family itself could be."

By & by Butler was mentioned & Fortress Monroe.—(these people lived, & live at Portsmouth), & never saw I anything to surpass the concentrated bitterness & fury with which *she* talked of him & his doings.[41]—She looked,—but *talking* & *looking* were almost equally expressive.—After a little further discourse of the war, & the changed condition of things, & the "N.Y. truck farmers about Norfolk" & the altered estates—On which I said absolutely not one word.—She suddenly & violently broke out—"I prefer not talking about the war,—it is cruel to mention it.—*I* cannot talk about it,—it made me & my section suffer too much.—*I* refuse to talk about it."—

"Excuse me, madame," said I "if I remind you that *you* began this conversation & have carried it on,—that *you* have said all that has been said about the *war,*—that *others* suffered as well as *you,*—that it was *your* section that was the aggressor, as *you* have been today, & that if any generosity has been shown in the listening to disagreeable sentiment it has been by me, not by you,"—at which she simmered. She settling into her seat, & I into mine,—but at last her curiosity or interest grew too great for her, & she fell to amicable discourse once more.

—About these same truck farmers amongst other matters.—They have bought all the decent land about Norfolk & are doing a thriving business,—the only Northern people of whom I have heard so far, in the South, who have held their own.

For the last of the ride to Norfolk we ran through a part of the "Great Dismal Swamp,"—which here is *swamp-y* enough, but not very dismal since in most places the trees have all been cut away.—It was in this & the adjoining county tho' that Nat Turner's insurrection was seen,—& so was full of suggestions if not of sights.[42]

—It was too late when I reached Norfolk to do more than take a little tramp through the town, with its narrow streets, & quaint looking houses, & lazy & sleepy looking shops & people. There is one old church, having its date on it in big iron letters 1759—& a cannon ball of the war of 1812, embedded in one of the walls.

I had a skimpy audience—of course,—but it was better than those at Richmond & Petersburg,—& a delightful one to talk to.—That queer being Emma Stebbins—(the sculptor) was there—sent me some lovely flowers, & had quite a talk with me after the lecture.[43]—She was putting up a stone over her brother's grave, who was killed near here.—I enjoyed the talk but it put me to bed very late,—& as a fiddle scraped all the rest of the night at a miserable dance hall opposite, & I had to be called before it was fairly light my sleep was abbreviated.

Getting down to the boat we passed the funny little market that amused us so in /65—but now it was quite deserted,—too early for even the market folks to be astir.

It is vile the way they call one here.—From the time we were called, & got across the river in the little ferry boat, & found our train & got *away* on it was *two hours & a half!*—An *hour* would have done quite as well.—Then when we were started, we ran only about 20 minutes when we stopped for breakfast.—Why we shouldn't have had the half hour elsewhere,—at Norfolk or Portsmouth, to have eaten a proper breakfast—with a later start—is one of the things that "no fellow can find out"—except indeed the R.R. people, who probably have one of their own creatures to keep the little den at which we stopped.

I couldn't help laughing at the darkeys who waited

on us.—They had their old habit of doing *one* thing, & one thing alone would they do.—One fellow came in with a huge tray, holding hominy, & planted *it* at each place,—another with something else.—Even the sugar & milk came separately,—You couldn't induce one of them to bring you anything for which you asked—or anything but just what had been entrusted to him, & the result was, we had nothing to put with anything else till it was time to decamp to the train.

I began this letter at Raleigh,—have scratched away at it here & there,—& yet, tho this is the 22nd of April, & Columbia, I have only got to an eating house just out of Norfolk.—I have tried & tried to write, but I have gawked & gawked so at everything when I have not been in the cars, as to entirely prevent my getting anything on paper.—I will write this evening of *myself,* & my marmee more,—but *must* send this now, just as it is.—Meanwhile & always I send Marmee my heart.

Macon, Georgia

4.28.1875

My dearest Marmee,—If I were to take thee from Norfolk to Wilmington, even in imagination it would make me tired for thee.—As much as I had heard of the "pine barrens" & the "dismal swamp" of Carolina never did I dream of the reality.—All day long we rode, from early morning to nearly seven in the evening crossing the entire width of the state, & saw nothing but dreariness, dirt, poverty, brutishness, & desolation.—An unbroken unending, seemingly endless continuance of indifferent looking pines,—no grass, no undergrowth to them, the soil out of which they grow a dismal, dingy white sand,—the trees scrawny as to growth, & every one of them cut & shingled about the base for turpentine—bled to death for it apparently. Scarcely a single clearing. Here & there in the trees a wretched hovel of logs & clay, or of blackened timber,—one or two rooms, carpetless, almost windowless, filthy,—a wretched little shed,—with perhaps a bony cow, which served as cow & mule both,—a ruffianly evil looking man, a yellow, skinny, bedraggled looking woman, & a host of wretched little scarecrows of children as inhabitants,—or else a perfect museum of ragged darkeys.

Again, here & there, we would come to a station,—a half dozen, or dozen of these cabins or houses (all of them with huge outside chimneys) a half hundred of these wretched, squalid looking people, white & black, big & little,—the entire town apparently turned out on the platform to see the train, the most of them without sufficient back bone to enable them to stand straight & so, hands in pockets, hitched up against & apparently glued fast, by their filthy rags, to the wall of the station,—such of the platform as they did not occupy strewn with bags of guano, which *everywhere* in this country is to be seen & *smelt,* making as satisfactory an odor as the dead fish in which we used to delight on Long Island.—A half dozen funny little two wheeled waggons standing about, their "tram" being a poor, little pathetic looking yet comical looking cow or steer.

All & all the people were the most utterly helpless, ignorant, "lousy" degraded, nerveless, limp, slimpsy,—& yet in many cases vicious looking creatures it was ever my bad fate to behold.—The pines, the soil, the houses, the people keeping on as they did all day without *any* intermission or any relief, or any *suggestion* even of better things depressed me so before night, as to make me actually melancholy.

Alas & alas for a Republic with such elements within it!

Also the heat & the dust were frightful.—I was nearly smothered, & powdered quite white all over, while the heat was so close as to be sickening.

We reached Wilmington at quarter of 7 & got into a carriage to drive about for half an hour to see the town, & the town coming on top of the country nearly finished me.—When I think of it now it is like a nightmare.—The same sand, with very few trees,—the sand so heavy as to let the wheels sink & sink as they might in *grit,* [some] of it flying,—a filthy slate color—no sidewalks to speak of,—very few even pretentious houses, & these black & "stringy" looking. The body of them wretched frame shanties,—one solitary white school house, & one long, low, shambling place—once a hospital,—the colored school.—very few women to be seen (which seems to be the case in all these Southern places) & these the usual *slinkey* looking ones,—a universal air of stagnation, & a positive suggestion of ruffianism & crime.—It makes me feel as tho' a nightmare possessed me only to think of it.—I was actually thankful to find my room at the hotel was on the third floor, or I should not have slept, I should have really expected to be murdered before morning.

There is a good deal of shipping here,—the business of course being turpentine & rosin, & there might be a busy stir if there was *any* stir to these same—paralyzed wretches.

Of course their debt clogs them, since the poor house of a state rejoices in a debt of about $56, to $58[,]000,000,—which they are at present arranging to repudiate,—the first step by the last legislature being an offer to pay 40 cts on the dollar, at the rate of about 2 or 2 1/2 per ct in 30 years in place of dollar for dollar at 5 or 6 per ct,—when they get *that* settled they will probably repudiate the whole thing in toto.—They certainly would if it all belonged to Northern people, for they manifestly whine that to rob, swindle & steal from a Northern man or woman is but a legitimate means of repairing the injury *we* did them. They have but one way of reckoning *everything* here, & that is before—or after—the state went up (that is seceded),—or "before or after the war"—& along the lines of Sherman's March it is "before or after Sherman."—They know next to nothing, all of these Southern people,—they have almost no schools, even the best of the houses are & always have been entirely destitute of books,—an immense mass of them cannot read (in N.C.

alone "before the war" there were 70,000 adult whites who did not know their letters) so that even their wretched little papers can give *them* no information,—as indeed they give *no* one.[1]—These are small, badly printed, filled with local advertisements often without a word of original matter, some stale jokes or anecdotes copied from old Northern papers, a greater column of telegraphic news from the N.Y. Herald, two or three days old, very few editorials, since the editors do not *dare* to say openly what they wish to say, but when they *do* write writing as blind leaders of the blind, or as wilful falsifiers.—The first, in most cases.

The whole South is where Pa. & N.Y. were sixty or seventy years ago with this difference—Those people *knew* what they lacked & were eager to gain it,—these people believe they lack for nothing & do not want it if it were thrust upon them.

Their stupendous vanity & egotism only equals their poverty of mind & estate.

With their impoverished lands, their hovels,—(their *palaces* are places a well to do mechanic would despise—the planter's palaces I mean,—without proper ventilation, with no means of heating but open fires, leakey & drafty,—without running water, without water closets, without *any* modern convenience, to say nothing of ornamentation, without pictures, without books, with some tawdry carpets, & gorgeous satin upholstery where they could afford it) *these* "domains"—not knowing how to cook, to eat, or to care for themselves, in this climate, marrying & inter marrying in their own county or their own family (their [. . .] when "before the war") it was considered absolutely *disgraceful* for a young man to go out of his own county to find a wife) not trained to work or even to exercise,—in consequence of all these causes—presenting to the world, a sallow, sickly, spindling, dyspeptic, anguished, shivering, worthless set of men & women,—absolutely uninformed or misinformed about the outside world, even where they have money so absolutely without taste as to dress like [. . .] (somebody once said that the war was a mercy to the human race in *one* matter, it compelled all the Southern women to dress in *black*)—& yet with all this these people do not merely assert, but assert with full belief that they are not only "a brave, chivalrous & sensitive people" (which all their papers & all their speakers are externally repeating) but that literally & truly,—they are the superiors of *all* the rest of the world in mind, body, & estate.—The thing is laughable in itself, but it has been & is anything but laughable to the republic in its results.

—Well to get back to this *special* development,—we drove about the town in the deep, dingy sand,—& looked at the few respectable looking houses, & the abundance of cabins & hovels belonging to an about equal mass of poor whites & poor blacks,—& noticed, as everywhere so far—(& farther thereafter) the absence of women from the streets,—& wanted to get out, but had not the time—to the little national Cemetery,—"little."—Alas! there are in it 2057 marked headboards,—but the most of these cover more than one sleeper, even whose name is unknown.

It was the first time the great dingy opera house had been opened since the passage of the Civil Rights Bill, & there was a stir accordingly, of which I knew nothing till afterwards. It seems the negroes had made a sort of compact among themselves,—as they have done in a great many other places *not* to take action on the matter,—& so avoid all trouble, for the present at least.

Not knowing anything of all this, when I came into the dressing room, I asked the colored janitor—a very bright, wide awake mulatto—who informed me he had built him a little house & had $1600 in bank—"Better than the old days!" said I—whereas he showed *all* of his ivories in response.—I asked *him* whether there was "any trouble about here over the Civil Rights Bill."

He "done reckoned not,—but dere's *one* [picture] dat stuck *hisself* up in his circle (dress circle) an tinks he's good as white folks for *shore.*"

I didn't understand his indignation at the time, till I found out about their compact, & that they felt this man had broken faith.—As I could make him out, from the stage, he was a very dark, very well looking & fairly dressed man, who had held I was informed, divers and sundry offices.

Afterwards Bernard told me that the man came up & asked for a ticket,—he handed him out a fifty cent one (*gallery* ticket) without any words,—the man handed it back saying he wanted a seat where "the white folks sat."—& Bernard, of course, without any more ado passed him a good reserved seat, & he put down his dollar & disappeared.

Directly, B. said, there came rushing down the stairs the proprietor of one paper, the editor of the other, & about a dozen of the citizens & citizenesses who pride themselves on their "position," & raised a yell.—"That nigger!" "Had he sold a ticket to that nigger because he *wanted* to?"—"Had he *chosen* to have that nigger in the house."—"Did he let that nigger go in on his own free choice?"—Answer! Answer!—clamor clamor!—Yowl! Yowl!

"Did he sell the ticket because he chose to?—Yes he did, ["]—smiling blandly—["]Yowl! Yowl!! Yowl!!" "He professed to be a law abiding citizen."—More bland smiling.—"He didn't *make* the law, & he didn't propose to break it."

Chorus of howls.—"The fellow *must* be put out,—*should* be put out."—"All right, ladies & gentleman" said B.—"*put* him out, if you want to, & are anxious to hand over damages, but if you think *I'm* going to pay over a $500 fine in your behalf you've made a slight mistake in your man.—I don't love you well enough for that."

Double chorus of indignant hoots.—Silence.—small consultation.—"Stay in the house" (they would have staid with perfect equanimity if he had only been on the other side of the rail) "with that nigger! never! never!—They would go home, & immediately,"—"all right" said Bernard, & went on making up his accounts.—They waited longer & glared at him,—to which he paid no attention,—more wait more glare—at last,—" we want our money?"—"Money for what?"—asks B.—"Money for our tickets—" poking out their scraps with the numbered ends.—"You must be joking" remarks B soberly.—"You have bought your tickets, & used them,—been in the hall & found your seats,—& the entertainment's begun.—if you don't want to stay & listen to it, that's no concern of mine,—*only* you'll oblige me by just stepping out of the way of those people who want to get up to the ticket office."

More glare,—more rage. More suppressed yowl, more consultation, then one & all meandered back, & sat, outwardly at last, like lambs, till the "entertainment" was over.

You wouldn't catch one of these people throwing away a dollar ticket!—Not much!—their indignation & their "chivalry" & their "honor"—spurious & *true,* (if they have any of the latter) they will all put into their pockets for the sake of a little gain.

Bernard thought there would be an awful howl in the next morning's papers about the affair, but there was not a word—only a very fair notice of the speech.

Which reminds me that I didn't tell thee about his "tiff" at Norfolk. When he was paying his bill at the "Landmark" office (one of the oldest & bitterest papers in Va) the Editor said—"Miss Dickinson isn't the sort of person I thought she was."[2] "What sort of a person did you think her?" inquired B.—"Oh a middle aged ugly, masculine,—Woodhull—freelove sort" answered he of the quill. "That's what we all thought her."[3]

"You must be a well informed lot," remarked B.—"Do you never read the newspapers—they've been full of her for a good many years.—"

"Yes, we read the newspapers—yes we read the newspapers! What then!"—bristled the editor, as if B. had spit on him.

"Well"—drawled B. with his aggravating air of simplicity,—"you *must* read them with *intelligence* then."

"What do you mean sir," growled the dignified leader of public opinion.—"Do you mean to insult me.—Let me tell you *we* don't stand that sort of language *this* way.—We have *killed* men for saying less than that."

"Yes" I know, politely assented B.—"That is the reason we sent an army down here.—Perhaps we'll send another one,["]—after which the irate editor had no more to say.

They are a set of barbarians.—"Scratch a Russian & you'll find a Tartar."—Scratch one of these "gentlemen" & you'll find a compound of savage & bully, & the bully simmers down when he finds you are not afraid of him.

Bernard[']s Democracy has been changed to ardent Republicanism.—"If Congress wants to convert the whole North,["] he says, "it had better make an appropriation to send every northern voter down this way, for a month. *They'd* go home sound enough!"[4]

The landlord (Davis by name) of our hotel (the Purcell House) was a vile looking, bullet-headed, red, haired, burly, brutal beast.—A Northern [renegage?].—Used to be an overseer, & slave leader, & looks it through &

through.—There was a young man on the coach,—a collector of bad Southern debts,—from the west,—had been an express agent on the plains & in California, & served through the war,—a slender, dark, dangerous looking chap, who kept exchanging "civilities" with Davis in an edifying manner.

It seems they had had a row in the dining room, to begin with. The young fellow could not eat his breakfast & had put it into a bit of paper to carry away when Davis stopped him, & informed him he must have it, or pay $1.00 for the "lunch"—whereupon they nearly came to fisticuffs.—Afterwards in the office they had another row over his bill,—& over ours.—We were in too late for B. to eat his supper so he said he would have it with mine, & ordered the two for our return. When we came back Davis had been absolutely beastly about it,—refused to have any prepared, refused to hear anything about its having been ordered,—informed B. that supper had been prepared at the regular time, & wasn't going to have any other for "any God damned stuck up's of fools who didn't know enough to eat at the regular time."—B came to me with the result, tho' not with the *details* of the interview, & we sallied forth to a wretched little restaurant to find something.—The next morning we left too early for [. . .] for breakfast, & did not go into the dining room at all.—So that our hospitality at that inn consisted of a night's lodging, & plenty of abuse, for which we were charged $12.50.

There was a constant *fear* in the coach,—the southern people not venturing to *say* anything openly, but looking as if they would like to stick knives into all of us. At last Davis said to me.—(I had not opened my mouth)—"nice streets to drive over, ain't they?"—"Sandy"—said I, looking at the foot-depth of dirty, gritty stuff through which we were sinking.—"That's so,"—said he, as if I had paid it a great compliment—"nice & clean.—No clay here.—Water doesn't lie on *this* soil.—Its just as dry & and nice to drive over after a rain, as if it hadn't rained atall."—The dark young man smole at me.—"contentment a great thing," said he.—"Yes," said I,—& smole in reply.[5]—

Davis hadn't the sense to see what we were driving at, but he bristled at every word that was said anyhow,—& after some more sparring all round, he said to me.—"You had a *re* markably fine audience last night["] (I had about a hundred cabbage heads.—) "I reckon you speak to *larger* ones—*sometimes,* north, but these are ra'al high toned ladies & gentlemen,—hard to beat."—"I should hope so," said I.

"And that opera house.—That opera house is the finest in the whole South outside of Orleans.—we're proud of that opera house, I reckon you haven't seen anything better in the South."

"No" said I. "Not in the *South.*" (it was a dingy, dark, forbidding looking hole, but ample in size of stage & audience room.)

"It might be that, & not much there," commented the dark young man.

Whereupon Davis & two other "natives" began,—"Its not *our* fault." "Its no fault of *ours.*" "Before the war things were very different." "We made a better show before we were robbed of everything," & c & c.

"Certainly" said I, "all the halls I have seen, &, as far as I know all the halls in the South belong to the *ante-bellum* days,—is that so?"

—"Yes"

"Well," said I, "I don't see how Sherman,—or the war, or the "robbers" had anything to do with them then." Whereupon there was a promiscuous growl.

All of their filth, ignorance, laziness, & poverty are put

upon the "invaders" & "the enemy"—They all lived like Solomon & she of Sheba, before "Sherman" & the Yankees came down.—Also, there is never the hint of a suggestion in anyone's mind, that they *began* the war.—We began it, & we are responsible for all the ills that even befell them from the days of 76 till now.

When we got to the cars there was another scene.—All three of us were going to *Columbia,* & had so notified the clerk the night before.—Had asked about the time of leaving, & had been marked to be sent to that train.—So! When we got to the depot & into the car,—there was *no* train,—it had been taken off four days before,—not marked on the train table, of course *we* could not know, —& of course the clerk, & his lovely master knew perfectly well.—It was more of a game of *gouge.* You see every where here,—almost *every body* who travels is Northern, & we are all a lawful prey,—a dollar apiece from the hotel to the depot, in a wretched old coach.—The hotel thought it would take us down,—bring us back, & then take us down again to the night train,—so that it would not only be the better by a day's board from each of us,—but instead of having $3 of coach hire, it would have $9.

B & I were going to Raleigh & had given it up, on account of the exceeding fatigue of the ride,—but of course we at once decided to go on—the train leaving in about an hour,—& the dark young man said he would go to Charleston,—or would sleep on the road,—but he would not go back to that swindler's house.

Of course both the young men had something to say about the matter, as they would have had it to say to *any* hotel keeper, North or South,—& when Davis found we really were not going back & he had nothing more to expect of us, he broke loose,—never heard I *such* an outbreak.—It was hideous.—The wretch walked up & down in the middle aisle of the cars,—stomping, raving, swearing, *screaming,* threw his hat on the floor, beat his breast, called us everything he dared,—as *Yankees,* informed us he was a *gentleman,*—Yes by G—a *gentleman,* & gave an extra scream, & an extra swear to emphasize it. Bernard busied himself about the hand baggage as tho' he did not hear him.—The dark young man stood & looked at him, always keeping his face towards him, with a silent smile, but with his hand on his *hip pocket,*—which attitude seemed to have a beneficial effect on Davis—at least it kept him to the line of screaming and swearing.

By & by *I* said to the dark young man, in an ordinary conversational way,—"Did you ever read Uncle Tom's Cabin?"—"Yes" said he. "Remember Legree?" said I. "Yes" said he, with an appreciative grin. "He was a specimen brick of a Northern doughface & renegade,—& of all mean skunks who cursed this Southern country, *they* were the meanest."[6]—

The landlord had stopped his wild cat performance, when I began,—tho' he sputtered & fumed so as to almost burst, but he *had* to hear what we were saying tho' we were talking as tho' we did not know he was within a hundred miles of us,—I saw from his look *he* had read the book & knew what we were holding forth about,—presently I turned to him politely & said,—"Is your name Legree?"—"No" he roared—"Got any relatives of that name?"—"No" he roared again.—"Oh"—said I.—["]I thought, perhaps, you were the brother of a man, my friend here & I were just talking about."—He looked tigerish, but the dark young man moved his fingers a little on that *hip pocket,* while we both looked at him in a friendly fashion,—& presently the beast growled his way off the car.

To think of this wretch being the absolute master of hundreds of human beings.

Well we went our way to Raleigh, having to travel all the morning back over the same road we had crossed the days before.—Pine barrens—dust, dreariness, heat, & wretched human habitations, & beings as before.

The car was mostly filled by Northern people on their way from Florida, but there sat near us two Catholic priests Paulist Fathers,—& a half dozen or so of the "chivalry"—

The talk was about the Beecher case.[7]—All of the Southern papers have some thing to say about the case, never in the way of information, but always to show that the whole tribe is a vile tribe together; & that it is a perfectly fair sample of the entire state of things & people in the North,—& there have been no end of the praisings of the Southern "ladies" in comparison with the Northern ones,—that they never have anything to say about this filthy matter which the "Northern females" delight in discoursing of everywhere.

Well! here were Southern men & women together,—"the *crème a la crème* of that section, & here were two witty, well educated, voluble Catholic priests (both of them belonging to the "[Sile]"—natives of the state) who were serving as chief spokesmen,—& it was surely too much for endurance.—Such garbage & filth, & nasty suggestions would have been hooted in a Northern caboose, where any woman had been present.—Yet all these refined "brave, chivalrous & sensitive" people,—"high toned ladies & gentleman," listened, & applauded, & laughed till the tears ran down their faces.

At Goldsboro, where we dined the day before, B & I stopped again, & changed cars,—&, as we had had almost nothing to eat since the aforesaid dinner, we were compelled to eat its counterpart, in spite of dirt, grease, & the spectre of a nightmare of indigestion awaiting us.

All the afternoon we rode straight west, as we had been

riding straight north & south through the state, but found no variation in the pine wastes, the wretched cabins, the squalid people, the untilled ground, the cow waggons, the lazy wretches in rags "propped" up against the walls of the dingy stations & the smell of guano, pervading every thing.

Raleigh we reached at 5:30, & found a really pretty town.—Very fine even good houses,—still quite a number, with a dozen or so built since the war,—the streets rough, the sidewalks only *half* kept, but the greatest abundance of flowers everywhere,—& endless numbers of oak trees,—black oaks, white oaks, live oaks, water oaks,—oaks of all sorts, & all beautiful everywhere.—The streets, such as they were,—wide, & pleasant to look at.—The town built on ground like all that about it,—rolling.

The first thing I beheld as I was driving to the hotel was a negro "slave" gang I had almost written,—Convict chain gang,—a couple of hundred, marching from their work of stone cutting (for the new penitentiary) with armed guards at each "corner."[8]

The Tarboro house is the best house we have found in the South,—new, clean, airy, comfortably furnished,—obliging & efficient landlord & lady & good servants,—but the cookery, as everywhere in the South, *vile.*

Mr. & Mrs. Blackwell who keep the house, are Southern,—he was in the army, but is a *really* well disposed reconstructed man,—likes Northern people not *alone* for their money.—She seems as sweet as honey, as does her mother,—as do divers of the other ladies who were boarding at the hotel,—& had I judged from their manner to me, I would have gone away saying "how well disposed & really loyal these people are."—But one day, after I had been talking with them in the hall, I stopped in the parlor, at the top of the stairs, for a few moments, &, as I came out,—I heard Mrs. Blackwell say—"I'd like to see every wretch of a Yankee burned at the stake"—"I'd like to burn them"—responding one of the others.

And the whole thing, false smiles,—almost fawning on a merely transient traveller, seeming good will,—& deadly hate is a fair sample of the entire state of things here,—shown in ten thousand ways.

My house the [*sic*] regarded as a wonderful one.—I really had about two hundred people, but of course, I ought to have been overwhelmed since they were "the very first people in the place."—They did make very attentive & very enthusiastic hearers—& the hall, while it is not a good one, is a very brightly lighted & cheerful one.

I meandered about the town the next day, & found not a *solitary* public school (there is no regular school system in the state) a Baptist, a Presbyterian, a Methodist & an Episcopalian school,—part boarding, part day schools.—The grounds very pleasant,—those of St. Mary's—the Episcopal one, really beautiful, large, with a lovely green sward, & great old oaks dotting it,—the buildings, quaint, & grey & antique looking,—all of them, inside, like every other one of their kind in this section devoid of what we in the North regard as absolute essentials to simple comfort,—no pictures, very few books, carpetless, dark, close smelling,—& the school system, & books, & most of the teachers such as to have the girls very nearly as well informed as it finds them.

The market house is new, but ordinary looking, & the markets where we were then, nothing to look at.—Of course there were churches in abundance,—everywhere, —some of them quite old, & fine looking,—one of them old & very queer looking, with the steps going up to the galleries *outside* under a wide porch.

The State House is of grey stone,—the grounds about it prettily laid out, but very tangled & ill-kept,—high steps

& some pillars on the front face.—In the grounds on one side, a wretched bronze (imitation) Statue of Washington.—Inside the place looks as if it had seen rough usage,—the passage & stairways are very indifferent,—but the arches supporting the house, in the basement, are really noble in their solidity & strength.—The Library was closed but the Senate Chamber, & Hall of Reps was open (The House of Commons as it used to be called under the old constitution.) The carpets are dark & neat, tho' well worn, the desks & chairs are substantial & old fashioned,—those in the Senate Chamber having half high backs,—& of some dark wood, mahogany I think.—The galleries are supported by huge Corinthian pillars, but are stuck up to the ceiling, very narrow, painted white, & so steep, that it made me dizzy to look down from there.—I don't know how any one sits there.—"The ladies don't often come except for a *great* day,—only on Saturday, when pretty much all the *school girls* come."—In the one house is a bust of Calhoun, looking as all his busts look to me, as tho' he were cross-eyed,—& a very nice engraving of the old Washington Monument that was here, & was destroyed, I think at the time the original capital was burned,—& I believe that was about thirty years ago.—In the other room, a full length daub of Washington.

I went Friday evening to a white Methodist meeting—to see what some of the poor whites were like, since I had heard so much of the queer doings of the negroes,—& I beat a retreat long before the evening was over.

The church was a queer, rough looking place with plain boards showing on the sides, & rafters overhead.—flaring & sputtering oil lamps & candles serving to make darkness visible.—The preacher raved & tore a [. . .] to tatters, an exhorter—after him—raved yet more, & tore smaller tatters, the people sobbed, & howled, & here & there beat their breasts, & acted very like lunatics.—"There he is!—there he is! right in the midst of you.—Satan!—Satan!! Satan!!!—flee from him sinner,—flee to the altar, flee ere he seizes you as he may this night,—this hour,—this minute,—& drags your soul down to roast in hell.——Hell's a gapping for you,—hell's a gapping, a gapping, a gapping,—oh yes Hell's a gapping,—right there under your foot, out there in the congregation.[9]—Come away from it come to the altar."—etc etc etc ad infinitum.—The only *good* thing he said to my apprehension was when he asserted that "this yet town was nearer hell than any place he'd been in for a right long time."

The next morning I prowled round town again, looked afresh at divers places,—saw the "Governor's *Palace*,"—a red brick old fashioned place, not used for some years past, & left to broken window panes & desolation.—Then I went to the "Shaw University" (named for some Shaw manufacturer up in the Conn. Valley, who has given it a lot of money).[10] There are, as I think I told thee no public schools here,—this is a sort of academy for colored young men & women.—It looks new, & not very inviting, but is far in advance, of course, of what the most of them have at home.—The rooms are uncarpeted, but comfortable in their necessaries,—well lighted & ventilated.—The Supt. & teachers are of the scrawniest, severest, primmest, ugliest most forbidding New England type,—with whom duty—in all matters,—is always a business, & never a pleasure.—Disagreeable as it is well possible for people to be,—to *my* liking.—I have seen their type else where here, in the like places, & have heard Northern people say—"What a pity for *this* class of Northern people to be here instead of more agreeable ones."—but the truth is that a less cold, obtuse, self reliant & determined set of people, would be worried, & badgered & mortified almost to death, & be driven away in short order.

It is very absurd tho' to see the way they talk to & treat these colored charges.—There is enough native tendency to pomposity & "airs" & folly amongst these people without fostering such a growth.—But instead of calling them by their first names, & speaking of them as boys & girls,—& young men & women,—it is constantly "Miss Smith," or "Mr. Jones" & "young gentlemen" & "young ladies"—& all in the most [mincing] & really unnatural way.

One thing had struck me about the Penitentiary prisoners,—my view of the state had assured me there were more ignorant, lazy, & worthless whites than blacks, & reason taught me as many bad deeds must be done by them as by their sable brethren, but I noticed that all the members of the chain gangs I saw were decidedly [grimy] looking.—I asked one & another this sort of question, "How many prisoners have you out at the Penitentiary." "Oh—a good many,—200 maybe,—no,—more than that,—more like a thousand I reckon." (Which is about the style of "reckoning")—"any of them colored."—a pause,—["]well,—yes,—a few,—some."

"How many?"

"Well—not many.—I don't know"

No 2

"Got many prisoners out at the Pen."

"about 5 or 600."

"How many colored?"

"Some,"

—& so on.—I could not get a word of information, & so being determined I went out to the place itself,—a high log wall—stockade, about the place,—cabins within,—armed guards a plenty,—the stone house built as yet no farther than a foot or so above its foundations.—

Confab with the warden.—"How many prisoners have you here?" "Nearly 600.—591."

"Plenty of them darkeys I suppose."

"Oh Yes,—plenty—all niggers but 75," & I went my way with *that* bit of information.—

I believe it holds good through all this country that a negro *always* gets more than his deserts of punishment,—a white man very rarely gets any where near his due.—Even in Republican & Negro South Carolina the *Judiciary* is all in the hands of the old masters of the situation.

A gentleman who called on me, when I got back to the hotel, edified me by the extent of his information,—he was quite a well to do countryman, & a fair specimen of the better class of small land owners,—he found me "a Yankee"—"Yes" I said as you say *Yankee* here, for you call everyone north of Mason & Dixon's line *that.*—

"Mason & Dixon's line"—queried he,—"What's *that?*"

—"But" said I, "if you mean a Yankee as *we* use the word you are mistaken—I don't come from New England, I come from Philadelphia."

—"Why" said he, with a completely puzzled air,—"aint *that* a county in Massachusetts?"

I was due in Charlotte Monday night,—Salisbury, where was the companion of the awful prison pen of Andersonville lies between Goldsboro, & Charlotte, & I intended getting off the cars there & spending Sunday—I said so when I came back from the National Cemetery that lies a mile or so out of Raleigh,—when I had a sad yet pleasant hour.[11]—The cemetery has in it six acres with but 1161 men buried in it,—648 of these known.—Probably they died in hospitals of wounds, & so had their names kept.—The Supt was originally an ornamental landscape gardner before he was a soldier,—(the Supts are *all* veterans) & he has made of the place a most lovely spot,—The ground, itself, is a little uneven, & all over it are quantities of beautiful flowers, rare roses, & great blossom covered bushes, with quantities of young growing trees.[12]

I asked one of the ladies at the hotel some questions about Decoration Day,—& she answered, under the impression, as I presently discovered that I was talking about the 26 of April (Southern Memorial Day) when I corrected *her,* she said,—in perfect good faith,—& meaning no *personal* offence to me "Oh! You mean Nigger's day."[13]—I was talking about the matter to a very pleasant woman,—a sister-in-law of our old friend Cattrell,—whose husband is the architect of the new P.O. here being built,—& she explained to me, that on *our* Decoration day, there is no one here to put flowers on *our* dear dead heroes but the faithful negroes,—& that when there is an oration made, it has almost none but colored hearers,—so these well disposed Southern friends of ours call it "Nigger's day"—Mrs—I forgot her name, Mrs. Cattrell we will call her, has been here for a year with her husband,—a refined, lady-like, elegant woman,—& she says it has been a year of purgatory.—Her concealed, & half concealed & wholly revealed hatred, mingled with the ignorance, the vulgarity, the coarseness & vanity of these people making life anything but a "sweet boon" to the Northern sojourner.

They are cunning enough to be as sweet as honey to the "passer by"—if the passer by has money or influence, but wo' betide the passer by, if he or she pitch tent & remain.

I found at the hotel on coming back a character of whom I had before been told,—somewhat famous in all these parts,—a Miss Abby House, an old woman, well upwards of sixty, dressed in rusty black, with cowskin shoes, & an enormous frilled cape & poke bonnet.—She was & is a raving rebel.—She actually drove young men to enlist with her stick,—a great club of a thing she always carries with her,—& she travelled far & wide begging everything in the shape of supplies that could have been of any service to sick or wounded men, & *got* it to them, spite of orders or refusals, or camp regulations,—even "Bob Lee" as she informed me, never said nay to her.[14]

I should have respected the old woman's earnestness if she had not been so crammed with ignorant spite, & furious hate & spleen—She knew *nothing* of the Gov.—she thought Pennsylvania was away off some where in the west, she had no ghost of an idea of why the war was fought, she believes it is not ended, & hopes yet to see the "torch put to the house of every mean Yank living."—She has not even any *Southern* feeling but just "Ca'lina."—*Gen* Johnston is a great man with her because he commanded in that department,—but Lee is no more than "Bob" Lee because he hails from elsewhere.[15]—They told me I would be amused & interested in her, but I was only disgusted.—She showed, with great triumph her stout stick, which was split in two up one half of it,—she having *broken* it an hour before over the head of a "sassy nigger"—one of the tidy servants in the house.—"That's the sort of Civil Right Bill they all ought to have," screamed she,—& all the "ladies & gentlemen" in the room laughed & were delighted.

Well! as I was saying, when I came back from the Cemetery I dropped the remark that I was to stop at Salisbury, & straight way was fallen upon by the landlord—the landlady, one man & another,—one woman & another to ask *why* I stopped?—a horrid place! no views,—no hotel,—nothing to eat,—nothing to see!—And then I got there at such a dreadful time!—four o'clock in the morning neither one thing nor the other—I would be tired to death!—To see the Cemetery?!—Oh! well,—but it was very small,—*very* small,—not as large as the one at which I had just been,—& not nearly so pretty!—

I smiled to myself,—a bitter enough smile it was too at the sudden & wonderful interest of these people in my doings & my comfort, where *Salisbury* was concerned.—"I don't wonder" thought I "that they want to dissuade any *seeing* eyes from going there!"—but they so steadily insisted that the Cemetery was *small* as to make me wonder & question with *myself,* at least.

All the same I went my way, leaving Raleigh at 5.P.M. & brought with me, for thee, this Confederate money which thee will see has been utilized as an advertising medium (the trains on this road are vilely arranged as to time) & Bernard & I had a long confab, & a very interesting one with a Dr Memminger,—the old State Attorney—a "carpet bagger" from Brooklyn who has been here ever since the war.

We parted at Greensboro (or Goldsboro I forget which it is) & *we* went our ways B to Charlotte,—I to stop off at Salisbury.—B went into the smoking car, & by & by came back to "communicate"—He had all along felt badly about my stopping at Salisbury, both because of what he heard of it & its hotel, & because of the *time* I reached there.—His presence being absolutely necessary at Charlotte.—But he was quite full when he re-appeared.—The conductor, & "another man" had been telling him what a poor thing it was to stop over for—the Cemetery—["]such a little one,—one of the smallest in the South,—etc etc such a *bad* arrangement for Miss Dickinson."

"See here my young friend" said I to Bernard "how well,—judging from our experience of the last fortnight,—do you think these people, generally, love me?—well enough to stick a knife into me—or to cut my throat?"

"That's about the figure" he answered.

"Well then" I demanded "why should they be so specially interested in my comforts & discomforts of travel at Salisbury, save that there is something there, they do not wish me to see."

"That's so," asserted B. All the same I puzzled & puzzled over what it could mean that one & all insisted on the Cemetery being such a *small* one.

Four o'clock came, & B reluctantly saw me into an omnibus at the station & went his way back to the train,—I went mine to a particularly villainous hotel,—but the omnibus "conductor" who was the porter, saw that I had some towels, & hot water, & put me into a room without my having to wait,—no one else was up on the shabby habitation. I left word to be called at half-past ten, & to have a carriage about an hour later, so at half-past eleven I went down & found an *ark,*—an edifice so queer, so shambling, so antique, so rickety, it smelled of the flood.

Even then,—in the town,—in its one solitary equipage,—ready to start,—the clerk & a friend of his watching me said—"Going to look round."

"Yes.—to look round the town,—& the old prison pen & the Cemetery."—

"Not much to be seen there"—they asserted as I drove off.

What *could* it mean I thought as I drove through the dingy, gloomy, low [bowed] houses, & the forlorn streets of the dismal town.—What *could* it mean.—*Everybody* says it is "small."—Can I have been mistaken all these years. —Salisbury was a horrible place, yet after all it *must* have been on a much smaller scale than I thought.—*How* could I have been for so many years wide of the truth.

So thinking I went away out of the town to a bit of a hill to the South of it.—Nothing on it now, but two choked holes that were once wells,—& an ordinary ploughed cotton field.—"The Prison Pen"—Whatever it had seen &

known of human agony it now gave no sign or token,—not a vestige of what had been, *was*.

From it I winded my way westward down a little slope & then up a new one not quite so high as the one I had left, & I turned my eyes quickly to the Cemetery.—Plain in sight,—sloping.—Yes, it was true, I could see the stone wall about it, & it could not by possibility compass more than six acres.—And all the front of the slope was clear—no graves,—& back of the Supts house I could see but a few hundreds of white head boards gleaming.

What did it mean? What *did* it mean?! I almost seized my head & held it in my troubled wonder.—Had my soul & the souls of millions more been harrowed for years over a *lie?*

We drove up the open space—more than half of the little grounds, to the Supts house, & he came out, a fair haired, fair faced, one armed, noble looking fellow.—"This is as it should be" thought I, as I looked at his right stump, limp & empty.

He talked with me for a little while, & then I, curiously vexed, & yet relieved said in a quite cheerful not to say airy tone,—"How many men have you here buried?" And his answer came,—slow & solemn & terrible—"Seven thousand one hundred & twenty five."

The awful surprise of the thing stunned me.—I could not speak for a little while.—Then I said, with my new mistake not quite gone away from me,—"Where did these men die."

"In yonder prison pen." "*Some* of them were shot?" —"*one* man lies here who was shot, &—he an escaped prisoner."

[A small sketch appears in the letter at this point offering a very simple map of the cemetery showing two squares of graves and a large open space between them.]

What *did* it mean.—I thought,—the tears coming into

my eyes none the less.—All about me I could see there were but a few hundreds of graves,—& I could see that but "*one*" Unknown U.S. soldier was buried beneath.—How to read the riddle.

"*How* many men are buried in these graves?"—queried I once more,—not noting that my query was in another *form.*

"425" he answered. 425—I thought,—am I going mad!—didn't he say "Twelve thousand one hundred twenty five,—& as I mused—in standing where the two little straight lines are our backs turned to the green, intervening space between the corners filled with graves—Mr. Richardson, my guide, said—"Will you go over to the trenches?"—

"To the trenches!"—I turned cold, & shook with a horrible chill from head to foot,—to the trenches.—Yes there they were,—eighteen (18) in a row,—four hundred & twenty feet long, crowded close together, filling such a little, little space,—without mark save their own swell under the grass & clover.—12,125 in the grounds here,—425 in the graves,—there in this sorrowful & terrible handful of earth eleven thousand, seven hundred & twenty heroes & martyrs, graveless, stoneless, nameless lay buried.

"Out of these twelve thousand one hundred & twenty five how many are known?" said I.—"93,"—he answered.—Oh! It was too much,—*too* much, I thought I should have died where I stood.—Twelve thousand & more, dead.—Dead not in battle, dead not where man can be confused with man, & a brother bury his own disfigured brother, not knowing him in his change & disfigurement,—but where name & place could be so easily kept.—More than twelve thousand men *starved* to death & of these who "held fast the profession of their faith without wavering" but *93* known.

Twelve thousand gone "out of sight & out of reach of hands,"—not merely their *graves* unknown, but they themselves unknown even the mothers who bore them not knowing *where* & how they ended their days.—A merciful want of knowledge tho' to *them.*

A. D. Richardson was in this prison, & while here, he kept a list of those of his companions who died but he soon escaped, & save this no record was kept at all.[16]—All day long the dead cart ran down the slope of the one hill, & up the slope of the other.—The trench was deep dug,—into it, till it was filled, our boys were flung like cord wood, twelve & fourteen deep, till it would hold no more, & then another was begun.

"I take the negroes testimony with caution" said the Supt.—Still sifting it thoroughly, "I have no doubt that many & many a man was flung in here while he was still alive."

In 62 when this hill was first opened there was a reasonably decent officer in command,—but he soon gave place to Maj Gee,—who, with his right hand Sargent Harris, & his officer of internments, Maj Meyers [*sic*] made a trio of devils incarnate.—Maj Gee was once asked "whether he had *not* the rations to give to the men."—& he answered "Yes.—He *preferred* giving them *quarter* rations."[17]

Through all the last of the war, this place was so awful that even rebel soldiers from the front were not allowed to go inside it.—lest even they should mutiny, [or] help these poor wretches so to do.

And yet it is useless for the officers in command to try to escape the odium of this hell—house.—All the civilized world *knew* that sickening horrors were here being enacted.—*They* knew as well.

Useless too for the people of the town to screen themselves as they now do behind the plea, "that they did not know"—& "even if they had known the place was under military power & they did not dare to interfere."

The pen was on the highest ground anywhere near.—When the first men were brought they were put into an old cotton gin,—but when that house was full, & another that was built the men were all heaped into the open space, with a stockade only about them,—a plank walk outside for the sentries,—the dead line ten or twelve feet within the fence.

I met one of the two union women of the town who gave some information about this.—And yet these women were not *union* women.—They were simply human creatures, who could not bear these horrors without trying to ease them by their small aid,—one, Mrs. Sarah R. Johnston smuggled food to them when she could,—&, rebel as she was, harbored one poor dying fellow in her house, & buried him with her own hands in her little garden, & had to fly for her life.—She got to Washington & Mr. Calfod helped her to Cin., where she now lives,—she had had enough of the South.[18]

The other, my informant, was supporting herself by teaching music at Raleigh, but was visiting a daughter here.—

"The plank walk was the favorite promenading ground of the *ladies* of the town for a long while.—From it they could look directly over, & see all that was going on of misery the other side the fence.—No shelter for the greatest number of them. No trees. No shade. They would, with their hands, scoop holes in the ground & bank up the earth & clay over them as a sort of roof, under which they would crawl.—Sometimes they would take one of their scanty garments & fasten over the whole & the clay roof as a sort of awning,—no clothing given them if they succeeded in living for months, so that they were often almost entirely naked.—Wells easily dug with the water lying near the surface, but shot dead if they attempted to dig more than the two opened,—& so they were parched often for water to drink & never had any to clean themselves,—"till they were copper colored."—"& yet" said she "I heard one of our clergyman say to another "The filthy wretches,—why don't they clean themselves." "Clean themselves" said the other with a laugh,—"They have so much dirt they are stuck together by it,—if a man here washed himself, he would be very apt to fall to pieces."

"Again & again" she said "I made great kettles of soup & sent my darkies up with them, with orders that they were to pretend to sell it, till they should get in.—& the officers in charge would laugh,—& taste the soup, & then pour it out on the ground at the gate."

"The darkies, who drove the dead carts, & brought in the wretched fire wood & rations, would conceal corn bread—all *they* had, in the mane of their horses, & when they got in pretend to be doing something about the horses heads & so untie the poor little shreds of food & let them drop."

Our government tried & tried to relieve these men, when it was asserted that the South was too poor to feed them—& when Stoneman came here in his raid of the winter of 64 & 5 he found heaped up outside the prison, where men starved & died by scores daily, *provisions to feed 20,000 men* for a *year*.[19]

And as to these wretches in the town, & their "military law"—if our government *could* have enacted such deviltry at any of its military prisons—Elmira for instance, the people of the town would have gone out enmasse to have fed them, or set them free.

And if they had any shame, whatever in them now, they would go out & tend these trenches, & on Decoration day at least cover them with flowers,—but as Mr. R. told me he lives absolutely alone, save for his darkey boy, & an occasional stray visitor.—No one had been there before me for months, & no living creature from the town ever comes there.—He is alone with his dead.

When I went away from them, & from him, & through all the rest of the day, I sat in my room like one in a dream.—There was such a weight on my heart it almost crushed it.—I could not go into the parlor where these people were, nor onto their streets,—I hated them with such a loathing as to make me *crawl* at only having to breathe the same air with them.

But by & by, just before I went, there appeared the "mayor & the whole town corporation."—They supposed I had been out to the "barracks?" The "barracks" consist of the one one armed soldier,—but I don't wonder they prefer calling the place by any other than its right name.—Salisbury has had a bad name,—from the prison,—which it does not deserve,—& they want Northern people & Northern capital to come there.—They are thoroughly reconstructed & loyal.—Oh yes,—*Want* Northern people to come there,—are friendly all round. Have buried the hatchet,—a good many Northern men *have* come there from time to time, & settled on the truck farms about."—So they gassed & lied—at last I said, "Have you any Northern men living here *now?*"—Well,—no, not exactly,—not *now.*—They had all done gone away."——————

"Oh!"——————————I guess so.

They all bewailed my not stopping here. Told me what a fine audience I would have, & some more of the same sort.—I was to be *impressed* for Northern service afterwards,—but I didn't impress much.—"If" I said at last. "Your paper here, speaks for your people, I think it is well I am not to test an audience."—Whereupon they shut up.—Here is the "elegant extract" to which I referred.[20]—

When the paper of this section was to get no advertising from me it has said its say with true *chivalrous* Southern fashion.—When it was to get even so little it put its "principles" into its pocket, & waded in in most complimentary fashion.

I almost stifled before six o'clock came, & I got out of that town,—& then, & now, & for all my life to come, I saw & shall see those long awful lines of trenches that epitomize so much of the satanic cruelty & the devilish degradation of human nature on the one side, so much of super human faithfulness & martyr devotion on the other.

Here are two little sprigs from one of the trees, & two little clover leaves from the trenches.—Put them away sacredly.

Even now, I can scarcely see how to write—nor hold my pen in my hand as I try to tell of it all.—I found at Charlotte a large & more prosperous town than Salisbury, but otherwise its counterpart. It has about 6000 people,—a few well looking houses, a universality of cabins,—a half dozen handsome places, so far as the grounds were concerned, with plenty of trees, & flowers, & shrubs.

B. F. Hill, one of the bitterest rebels in all the South, (once Gen. in the Southern army) lives here & edits a perfectly fiendish paper.[21]—His co-editor is a man who was known to have killed at least a dozen men, & who has served out a [K—K—?] term in the Albany Penitentiary,—Shotwell by name,—& the townsfolk think it is a very "good" name & like to make *loyal* puns upon it.[22]

The whole place is rank with secession.—There isn't a school in the place except two small boarding schools, & a quite large military academy.—Where boys & all dress in the regular Confederate grey uniform, & the professors are all old rebel officers.

We were scowled at when we went abroad as tho' we had been dangerous wild beasts, & the man who drove us would have been more than happy—from the way he behaved—to have broken our necks, if he could have done so with safety to his own.

Finally when we got back to the hotel, where we were scowled at by clerk & "clerkess" & people generally we were regaled by a specimen of "Civil Rights" in this neighborhood.

Three or four nights previous there came to this house, with his family (wife & child) a member of the S.C. State Gov. on his way home from some business at Washington,—very gentlemanly & well dressed & so white they let him pass unsuspected.[23] But almost an hour after he got in, & while he was in the dining room (the others being in their rooms) a rush was made on the place from the people outside, who, in some way had discovered who the man was.—The hotel keeper having the fear of the law before his eyes,—& a wholesome awe of $500 fine fashioned the front of the house so that the "respectable" mob could not get in,—enraged at that they rushed round to the back, & were going to make a promiscuous assault on everything,—but again the hotel keeper, being wise in his generation, turned off all the gas in the house—in a second, at the metre,—& the colored cook seized his opportunity to get the man away & hide him, & in hiding he had to keep for two days, when he at last got fairly away, & his family was sent after him.

"They might have made it as *lively* as they pleased for the nigger"—said the landlord "but I wasn't going to have my furniture destroyed.["]

The letter enclosed is one from the solitary morning paper—the Observer.—The bill was simply outrageous,—& as he announces in the P.S.—a "mistake"—the "mistake"?! More than doubling what was already preposterous, & yet he falls upon Bernard for not cheerfully paying it, because *they* haven't blackguarded me,—& because they *can* do so, if they will, tomorrow.

The extract is from B. F. [*sic*] Hill's paper.

Another *weekly* paper that had been *filled* with just such stuff before I came,—which of course then had a line of advertisements of mine, sent Bernard a bill of $12.50 for "notices"—the filthy abuse aforesaid,—of course he laughed at the thing & sent it back.

The next morning, as we were leaving the place, just as the train was beginning to move Bernard was arrested for $15.—the $12.50 for the paper, which he owed just as much as he owed it to Julius Caesar, & the & $2.50 for the Sheriff.—There was no time to parley,—no train for 26 hours (as is generally the case hereabouts) no body to look after things at Columbia where I *had* to speak that night,—& so under protest,—the sheriff, & everybody looking on understanding perfectly well that it was a piece of infamous swindling & blackmail—he paid it.—The sheriff made to sit down on the elbow of the end of my seat,—& I, speaking for the solitary time, said,—"Don't you sit down there,—don't touch me—you are as filthy as your work."—He looked like a whipped cur, & nobody about ventured to put their eyes straight before them,—but the thing being done, the sheriff was congratulated as he got off, with the train under almost full headway,—we have "done a right smart piece of business on the Yankees."—Tho' even the men on the cars, from the town, afterwards confessed to B. (in the smoking car) that this newspaper man was *known* to be a regular shyster & blackmailer,—next door to the jail very often,—not one of them interfered in *this* case,—one & all thought it was a good thing to get some money out of some Yankees.—Highway Robbery, & burglary are perfectly honorable in their eyes, as against a Northerner.—According to their reasoning the Gov. has stolen everything from them,—each individual Yank is responsible for the "stealing" of the gov. & a thief in his or her own right, & so lawful prey.

This is the town where they are to hold their "Centennial"—of the Mecklenburg Dec of Ind. 20 May, 75.[24]—The most ridiculous & preposterous & "*ugly*" of claims.—It is very like that *such* a paper could remain in absolute obscurity till 1819—*44* years, & *then* have nothing to show for the "original," but a *copy*.

The whole thing is simply a "Confederate" blow out.—Gen. Jo. Johnston is to be chief master of ceremonies,—the leading visitors & orators are all to be leading rebels,—& the call on all sides is for the troops to come up, & to make the day a glorification of those who fought in the *second* war of independence, quite as much (& a deal more) as for those who (ostensibly) proclaimed for a first.

The President was invited, but *not* by the regular Com.—of course with the understanding that he would decline, that they might have the opportunity they now have, of "howling" at him.

Glad were we to get away.—The country all down the line of the road, almost to Columbia—through S.C. is like the greater part of *western* N.C.—In place of sand, a bright red clay soil, that nevertheless produces good cotton, & reasonably good corn & rye (when it is worked.) &, in place of the flat region we had seen for days, there is quite a roll to the land, but everywhere there is the same squalor.—In S.C. we got into the region of the colored folks who are working their own small places,—& of those who are working the great places "on shares"—a very common method here, in place of wages,—&, while *any* sign of work & property in their case is a thing to be glad of, their horrid looking little cabins, poor scratched land, starved looking mules or cows dragging their "shovel" ploughs, were any thing but savory sights.[25]

Pine trees, & oaks everywhere abounded.—The pines without beauty,—the oaks *all* beautiful.—Among them a great number of *water* oaks,—growing in swampy & wet land, about Columbia in strike grey, sandy soil again.—

Here & there are a few "fine old houses,"—the fine old houses being low hovels, one story & a half places, built in the form of a Grecian temple, with an enormous, heavy, portico, or piazza put on along the front,—but the "places" about these houses used to be enormous, from a thousand to four thousand acres.

All of the places are lacking in any air of comfort,—big & little they stand on built up brick piles,—or on the ground, without a sign of a cellar, & must be full of ague & disease & fevers through part of the year, & wretchedly cold & uncomfortable in the winter.

And, indeed, very often *outside* of winter.—The day we were in Columbia it was bitingly cold, & the wind blew almost a hurricane.—The hotel is kept by a good Northern man, & is very well kept,—& I staid there spite of the efforts of the Chamberlains to induce me to come to theirs—however I took a long ride with them, & went up the next day to lunch. Gov. Chamberlain is the brother of my Chicago friend—Leander, & in some ways is very like him.[26]—

He is certainly doing a good work in laboring for a regeneration of the State, & dealing summary punishment out to the scamps who have so long preyed upon it.—Still

I think he is like to run to the wrong extreme, even in this.—He will find, if he is not *more* than careful, that the old rebels are simply using him to get such & such people & obstacles out of their way, & when they see a path clear, they will put him & his to the wall, & ride in again triumphantly.

I could not help smiling as I read his speech at Concord—or Lexington, a few days later.—His talk about the fraternal feeling & the rest.—Mrs. Chamberlain informed me, that tho' they have lived here for six or seven years,—& are what they are, refined, well disposed, elegant people, with no taint of obnoxious "carpet baggery" about them,—the pastor of the church they attend has never called on them, & not *six* people in the place,—who call themselves ladies & gentlemen, have ever been inside their doors,—no loss to *them,* since these people *are* so ignorant & narrow, & ill informed & vain, as to bore any reasonable Northern person almost to death,—but *that* has nothing to do with the *spirit* here.

Mrs. C. told me of some ladies being announced a few days before, rich members of her church, who called to ask her to solicit subscriptions from the other Northern members of the church, to not one of whom had these women ever spoken.

They were standing when she came in,—had seen her hundreds of times without ever bowing to her, & then announced that they had called "on business"—& stated it,—still standing.

"I will not ask you to be seated," then said Mrs. C. with great dignity,—"since you have called upon business, & have stated your business the business is done.—I have nothing to say to you but good morning."

And these impudent beggars went away in a towering rage.

Also these same ladies were going to have a Martha Washington tea party—& with it some tableaus.[27]—Mrs. Chamberlain is an exceedingly handsome woman, in face & figure, & these creatures came to her, to ask her to stand in the tableau as Mrs. Washington,—making a show of herself at so much a head, they to pocket the proceeds, while they refused to have anything to do with her socially.—Of course she would have done no such thing,—proud & refined as she is for *friends,*—& for these.—

And yet her refusal would no doubt be commented on with asperity by the beautiful New York Tribune as a "thrusting back of the olive branch"—& a waving of the "bloody shirt."[28]

Columbia in its prime must have been a lovely spot.—There are no really fine houses, but there are a good many presentable ones,—& the grounds about these are perfect,—filled with tropical flowers in tropical abundance,—shrubs, japonicas & magnolias, weeping cypress & the greatest variety of evergreen & sweet smelling trees.

The streets are very wide—the most of them 100 ft. with rows of trees on either hand, & a double row of trees planted down the middle of a great many of them, with a bit of green sward between.

There are here a great multitude of public & charitable buildings, schools & colleges,—but the most of them are dingy & ill kept, within & without,—some of them deserted, & the schools generally given over to the negroes.

The white people will not send their children to school with the colored,—the colored will go,—& the result is that this present growth of South Carolinians, is like to present a body of at least reasonably well informed colored people & of absolutely ignorant whites.

The State house is built on the plan of the Capitol, but without its majestic steps & porticos & pillars, & while it is correct as to artistic proportions, it has a very *flat* look. It is of grey stone, the under & the upper parts of the building being unlike, & the roof has in it some sort of tarry or oily matter that has run down & stained it,—niches have been left for statues,—but statues there are none,—Two large medallion heads are up on the front face, one of McDuffee & one of Calhoun, & in front of the building on a bit of open space, is an *iron* palmetto tree, so natural as to deceive the very elect.[29]—It is the work of a poor man in Charleston, who revealed the secret of his work to some rich man, & the rich man has made a stupendous fortune out of it, & the poor man still plods on.[30]

Inside the building is beastly looking,—the red brick arches are not even plastered (those supporting the building on the first floor)—the halls & stairways are of some sort of common wood that has held stains & dirt.—the Senate & Hall are indifferent looking, & absolutely without ornamentation.

It is curious to see the number of colored people of all shades, men & women, slaves ten years ago, who are not only well & elegantly dressed, but who carry themselves—not with the peacock shirt you often see in these people—but with real—dignity & air of command,—a great many of them have held, or do hold office, & the effect of that thing is seen in the negroes all through the state.—Elsewhere in the South, as far as I have seen, —specially in Georgia the manners of the darkies are very like those of slavery,—a certain subdued almost cringing air,—but in South Carolina they act like men.

My house at Columbia was the best I had anywhere & was a curious mixture of really elegant looking "rebels"—& equally elegant looking colored people.—Whatever they thought of one another they made no sign.—"Civil Rights" is an established fact in S.C.

Going to the cars the next day, Henry Purvis ran out to the hotel omnibus to speak to me.[31]—He had called on me,—while I was at the Gov's, & so had failed to see me.—When I found who he was, I said, "Come in, come in, & tell me about the people at home,"—so he scrambled in & we had a friendly chat,—no one was within save B & L,—& a very pleasant merchant from Albany, (of whom we afterwards saw a good deal)—except the train conductor & some hotel or baggage man.—Henry sat down by the conductor,—a big, red faced man,—opposite me,—& I could scarcely keep my countenance to see the fellows choking rage. He really looked as tho' he would have an appoplexy, if he could not let some blood—*ours* preferred.

At last Henry said something about his father's white hair, & of how well he looked,—when I said "Yes I think he is handsomer than ever,—& that is wholly unnecessary, for he was always, to my liking, one of the handsomest men I ever saw."—At which I really thought the conductor would have snorted himself into a fit, & fallen backwards out of the window.

At the cars, young Purvis said good-bye,—& our Albany friend told us that the conductor standing outside was literally *raving* to some people over the matter, & all the way down to Charleston, he behaved like an absolute brute.—Bernard at last came in from the smoking car, where he found himself alone, with the assertion that the conductor looked at him, & behaved in such way, that being unarmed, he was actually afraid to stay.—& at the supper place, he started the train seven (7) minutes ahead of time, simply because he thought we were in the supper room, & he would leave us at that lonely place for 24 hours,—but we had "suspicionated" him, & slipped out before we were done,—so he was balked of that sweet revenge.

The country we saw but little of as it was midnight when we reached Charleston,—but passing over it afterwards in the day time it was revealed as the same cabins, pines, "old fields" (as they call a place once under cultivation, now gone to waste) fields here tilled of grey soil,—dirt, poverty, & desolation.

Here I must stop.—I began it at Macon, & here I am at Nashville,—but I will write again tonight or tomorrow.—I am very, very sorry that I have been, of necessity silent so long, & that I have had nothing to communicate, save interest of travel.

I heard from home here, & very glad was I to hear,—& I will have B. telegraph tonight where I am to be next week,—somewhere in the *North* by that time, as I go from here to Evansville, Ind.

I have made my expenses,—& I have made literally & absolutely not one penny beyond that,—but I shall have some *fees,* next week or the week after.

Sorrow is no word for my regret over many things that are as they are,—but better times are ahead.—

I hope the long letter that was mailed thee at Atlanta, by way of Mt Vernon has reached thee, & that thee could read it.—If thee can't make this out,—for it is written in great haste, Julia Meyers will get through it for thee.—

I think of thee many many times every day,—& send thee my heart.

Anna

Nashville, Tennessee

4.30.1875

Dearest Marmee,—I left thee getting into Charleston, at midnight.—A bright moonlight night, through which the light stone & brick of which the place is largely built, shone cheerfully,—but as for us we were in anything but a cheerful mood when we reached the hotel,—for it was literally crammed,—& scores of people could not be furnished with even cots, but had to sit up all night.—The rush of people home from Florida, was & still is, so tremendous, as to overrun all the hotels.—At last, however, by dint of an awful *row*—ing on Bernard & Harmont's part (H. is the Albany gentleman) they succeeded in having one of the clerks dragged out of his room, & the place given up to me for the rest of the night.

What filthy beasts men—the most of them—are!—of course the bed was made up first for me, but I could not sleep in the place.—There was such a menagerie of hair oil, & grease, & blacking bottles,—& smell of dirty clothes hanging on the walls,—& such a generally nasty atmosphere as to keep me awake.—Early in the morning, the train being gone northward I was transferred to a very nice room on the parlor floor, looking out on the quadrangle.—Nearly all the Southern hotels of size are built about a large square court yard, filled with turf, & lovely flowers, & sweet scented trees, & singing birds.—A great comfort,—for the hotels themselves,—even the best of them are beastly,—stuffy beds, curtains, carpets, dust & dirt under them,—a sickening smell of rats & mice dead & alive in every room that has not its windows wide open.

After breakfast—(the 15 of April—I had been at Richmond 1, 2, 3, 4.—Petersburg 5. Norfolk 6.—Wilmington 7.—Raleigh 8, 9, 10. Salisbury 11. Charlotte 12. Columbia 13.—Charleston night of 14.—15.—Went to Savannah 16 & staid till morning of 21.—back to Charleston sleeping there that night.—Columbia 22, 23. Went to Macon aft. & night of 24.—Andersonville 25.—slept at Macon same night.—Atlanta 26. Chattanooga & Lookout Mountains 27 & 28, Nashville 29 & 30—where I now am,—at about the end of my Southern meanderings)—

Well, to return, after breakfast—the middle of April,—for which I feasted upon great store of delicious strawberries,—Mr. H & I sallied forth,—B. being too busy about his lecture business to go along, & Harmont proving almost as indefatigable a sight seer & class questioner as John himself.—We ran all over the place, losing ourselves, & finding ourselves, in fine streets & narrow streets,—into churches & graveyards, & theaters, & halls, & markets, & jails, & police headquarters, & warehouses & shops.—We interviewed citizens on the streets, & at the doors,—& were probably regarded as a couple of harmless lunatics, but really found out more & saw more than we could have done in a carriage & by ordinary means in a week.—The streets are reasonably wide, & fairly paved tho' broken in many places,—the side walks good,—a great many pleasant shade trees, & among these a good many of the green, spiked palmettoes. The buildings are nearly all of light brick, or light stone, or plastered, many of them with old fashioned, high pointed French roofs,—& the whole effect—in spite of the stagnation of business,—is of a bright cheerful city. The shops are fairly good, but with little going on in them, & there are traces of fire all about them.—Still it is remarkable how little damage was done by the tremendous amount of shelling.

In a great many buildings tho,—even inside on the ceilings & walls, you see traces of shells & balls, in the shape of mendings & plasterings,—& often by the things themselves still holding fast where they were imbedded.

I would go in to get some little thing, & ask the shop keeper about the marks, or the fixing,—& he would tell me, with a deal of bitterness, of how the "Yankees"—or "the *enemy*"—now & then "the federals" but not often—had shelled it, & what damage they had done.—Again, always, here as everywhere, the "Invaders" were responsible for the whole thing, had begun it, carried it on wantonly, & were generally wretches worthy of death.

I have yet to hear anywhere, our troops called "Union" or "United States" troops.—In Charleston, especially the old fellows, with high stocks & standing collars, discourse of "the enemy,"—with a magnificent roll to the words, edifying to hear.

At the P.O.—which is an outrageously shabby & dingy & contracted looking place, out of divers windows when we went up to inquire were thrust the faces of colored clerks, some of them black as ebony,—all of them quiet, gentlemanly, well informed—we asked them a procession of questions—&, as far as we could judge efficient.

We dived into the Charleston Library,—a queer little, old fashioned building, with antique entrance, & steep, wide stairs inside,—the library on the second floor, with a few thousand books, all of them pretty dingy & old, with antiquated scruffy librarian & assistant—talking & feeling as tho' they were inhabitants of the ark,—with some original letters & documents of Revolutionary time, framed on the walls, & with a plenty of fresh looking prints of Lee, & Jackson & Beauregard & their like & kind.

We went to the oldest church in the place—St. Michael's—Episcopal,—built in 1765,—& were amused at the young houses of pews,—huge & square & high backed,—some carpeted & cushioned, some not,—& all of them so tall as to enclosure as to hide the people from the minister & the minister from the people.[1]—one might well suppose,—& we gawked at the place where a tremendous shell had burst through the wall back of the altar, & had dented the pulpit steps & the floor in front of them when it fell.

The spire of St Michael's is the highest in the city & stands right in the centre of the *business* part, & was used as a landmark for our guns.

We saw a good many other quaint, old churches,—& finally, opposite St Philips, we stumbled upon a mossy, almost deserted little cemetery (on the other side of the street from the ancient church) with trees, & rank growth of grass & flowers, & wandering about in it we fell upon the grave of Calhoun,—at the time of the bombardment he was taken up & carried to Columbia, but the war being ended, he was brought back & freshly entombed.

Whether they thought the "Yankees," would rival them in fiendishness & break open his grave,—or whether they thought he was of such value he would be carried away as a sacred relic, I know not.

The tomb is a square raised brick thing, about a foot & a half or two feet high, covered by a marble slab, upon which, in large raised letters is simply Calhoun.—I send thee a rose from his grave—if thee cares for it well,—if not, drop it.—It is inside a letter which is a bit of a curiosity.—The request being from "Carpet baggers"—evidently *they* think they are to *beg* whatever they cannot steal,—& the notice is cut from the Carpet bag papers at Columbia, but the Gov. & all the best Republicans made such a row about it, that at last the Editor announced that *he* was absent & knew nothing of the article, & that the man who wrote it,—one of the state officers was too drunk to know what he was doing!—

Afterwards there were divers very handsome notices of me & my doings.

In our prowlings we went to some of the wharfs & saw a pretty little steamer go off with hundreds of queerly dressed Northerners,—the flag flying & a band of music,—& I innocently supposed they were going to Fort Sumpter,—but was informed that "scarcely any of the Northern travellers ever went over there."—How soon, & how *meanly* we are forgetting what has been done for us, & the places *where* it was done!

The City hall is quite the finest public building in Charleston, & we were shown about it by one of the city officials—a bright mulatto, a few years ago a slave here.—Now in authority—as well informed as he was bright,—a warm admirer of Gov. Chamberlain, & a disapprover of the Carpet bag stealings. The main room has in it a series of full length portraits of Revolutionary worthies, together with one of Calhoun that gives him a better face than any other portraiture I have seen of him.—Generally his face as shown is thin, hard, treacherous, cross eyed & forbidding.

The whole of the roof of this place was beaten in by the bombardment, & other damages done it—now, all repaired.

At the police headquarters we saw a gathering of white & black officers, in most amicable relations.—The police force of the city is equally divided between the two people.—The cells for temporary detention are at the back of this, & we saw some negro boys in them,—our colored officer, laughing & joking with them in a good natured way as he opened the doors.

I doubt whether discipline would ever be strictly enforced, or the laws be severely administered if the negroes had it to do against their own.—They seem to have the bitterest envy & jealousy of one of their own number who rises in the world, but the most amazing fraternity for one another in poverty, suffering or [. . .] of *any* kind.

After dinner,—with plenty more of strawberries—we went to Fort Sumpter.—The fort lies about four miles & a half, nearly due east of the city, at the mouth of the harbor, & there is no way of reaching it save by a large sail boat.

We sailed away past the island on which is castle Pinckney, past divers other islands, past Sullivan's Island with Fort Moultrie, none of them making much show for themselves.—These on the one hand, on the other "the hundred pines"—a group of dark, gnarled old pines, at the end of (James Island, I think) a relic of Revolutionary times,—the long low swamps of James Island on which were planted our batteries & guns, the famous "swamp angel" amongst the number, & the other long low lines of the sands of Morris Island, that were the arena of such desperate daring & heroic courage.

Fort Sumpter has but little trace of its original self. It covers the entire island on which it stands, with enormously thick walls of brick covered densely by sand—the walls I think are 15 feet thick, with double rows of guns on two sides of it, looking out to sea. The place was full of men, & ridiculous looking small mules hard at work in the thick sand.—The place is to be made as nearly enemy proof as place can be.—A bit of the old flag staff shows above the ground, & I got a scrap of it.[2]

Standing on its walls one can look across to Morris Island,—its *point* running out from the South, almost due east of it, not a mile away.

[At this point in the letter, Dickinson has sketched a small drawing showing the islands off the coast of Charleston.]

The island is five miles long, & all of it is historic ground,—but out at this extreme point is its immortal ground,—Here stood Battery Wagner, & here was done the work of Robert Shaw & his men of the 54.[3]

It was growing towards sunset as I stood & looked from the walls of the great fort, to the shifting sands that seemed but a stone's throw away.—The blazing light shone down on the barren glittering island, no tree nor shrub to be seen, as it shone on that close of a July day, never to be forgotten.—Whether it was a lack in me I know not, but the fort failed to move me.—What was *here* done had precipitated the stupendous struggle, but had been done without any real consciousness of all that was involved,—but what had been done *there,* was for liberty, for right, for justice for humanity, for a *redeemed* republic, & the men in doing & defining, as men almost never before did & died,—knew to the full for what it was done.[4]

I could scarcely wrench myself away from the spot, & its suggested memories & pictures, & the thoughts it compelled.—I wanted to go over to the island, but one cannot land on the point by reason of the surf,—& battery wagner itself,—& Robert Shaw who was "buried with his niggers" & these men themselves, have all been carried out to the sepulture of the great sea.[5]—The tides are constantly carrying away the shores of the island,—& *this* part has gone, save for a very little fringe of the fort.—So that these men who died for their country, have not, in their country, even a grave.

It was almost dark when we got back,—& I found in the hall—or rather the theater, where I everywhere speak—there are no halls,—a decent audience in point of numbers, & a very quick & pleasant one to tell my story to.

After the lecture we scrambled into an open carriage & drove through the delightfully mild & moonlit air—up & down the Battery.

The Battery is the Fifth ave of Charleston,—a long, irregular street,—following the water line,—the houses of course, only on one side, the beautiful bay in front,—on part of it trees & flowers, & pretty little walks & seats.[6]

The houses, are all picturesque in appearance.—Some in Spanish style, some French, some Moorish,—with verandas, & gables, & high roofs, & endless store of flowers & shrubbery about them.—Little palaces in the moonlight, tho' in the day they all show they would be very much the better for renovation, cleaning & repairs. The moon shone upon these,—upon the wide pleasant drive, upon the waters of the historic bay, out of which flashed lights here & there from Castle Pinckney, fort Moultrie, Sumpter,—some boats & ships at anchor,—the air was filled with the scent of magnolia blossoms & orange flowers,—& we went away, at last, tired as we were with infinite reluctance to bed.

The next morning we drove two or three miles over a cranky plank road to our little ferry boat,—in this to a vile depot—when we took the cars to Savannah,—& had a plenty of room.—There is very little travel going South. More grey looking soil, deserted places, "old fields" pines, half scratched earth with cabins here & there, more shabby looking, lazy looking people,—the *only* ones, literally & absolutely being at work anywhere, the negroes,—rice swamps showing here & there, & at last, long before we got to Savannah, great reaches of cane brake at which I looked with great interest.—I had often wondered how the slaves *hid* in it,—but seeing it wondered no longer.—It grows in the swamp,—a thick reed, with a head a little like a corn top, long skimpy leaves.—10 or 12 feet tall,—standing so thickly that the very stalks are *jammed* against each other.—Once in this no living creature could be seen,—tho' how any living creature ever got out of it is a mystery—& the water of the swamps threw off the scent from the dogs.[7]

Savannah we reached at two o'clock, & being there for some days I had a fine chance to see it,—& saw that it deserved its name—of the most beautiful city in the South.—The streets are very wide, unpaved & sandy, but with exhaustless beauty of trees in double rows,—& these streets are broken at every block or so by little parks & squares,—the street running round these, as round a quadrangle,—& these sodded & beautifully shaded,—there must be at least a hundred of these,—with one large one, on the outskirts, the very counterpart of Franklin Square, only twice or thrice as large—& infinitely better kept—Wright Square.[8]

There are a good many hospitals, & convents, & schools, & such places, all standing back from the streets, surrounded by low brick walls, like our Friends meeting house walls only not so high—& white washed—& these grounds are filled with flowers & flowering trees,—& the walls are over run with rose vines in full & sweet scented bloom.

—And there are at least a dozen old cemeteries,—full yet beautifully kept, with queer great brick tombs, as large as cabins, with tiled & sloping roofs, & a marble slab in front looking like a white door,—& other tombs & stones,—none of them crowded,—all standing with wide spaces of green sward & trees, & flowers between,—& with no fence walls about the lots,—& with the same low brick walls that are around the schools &c,—around all.

Georgia in the old days, was, I believe, the richest state in the South,—& is now,—& the houses testify to it. So large as to need a retinue of servants to keep them up,—& really handsome as to style & surroundings.

I went out twice to their famous cemetery Buena Ventura—famous simply on account of its moss & its trees. The ride to it is over a road made of oyster shells,—very hard & smooth, but frightfully dusty,—six miles out,—& you drive round this road in a sort of semi circle for some miles beyond the cemetery, where it again sweeps in to the line on which you have come out.—It is the one drive of the place, & all along it the negroes have got themselves little truck patches & put up for themselves cabins & bits of houses, to the unending disgust of all the chivalry,—as I heard it loudly expressed.—It is very difficult for a colored man, or a poor man of any kind to get hold of any land in Ga.—The effort is to keep large places intact, & to sell only to large purchasers,—so that far fewer of the negroes have their own places, than in S.C & Va.

Buena Ventura is a very large cemetery with a very few graves.—The trees are planted in double rows,—immense live oaks,—exceedingly old, making an arch over head as perfect as that made by the New Haven elms, but more sweet,—& from these depend millions of weepers of long, grey, weird looking moss.[9]—It is sad & solemn looking in the morning light,—& in the evening, as I saw it last, fairly ghostly.—I like it not.—I think the last resting place of our dead, for the sake of all survivors, should be as sunny, & flowery, & cheerful a place as it can be made.

I was glad to get in when I did.—As that afternoon there was a prize drill of the militia, & they went all out,—together with about the entire city.

A thing to instantly strike a Northern traveller, is how carefully all their military schools & organizations are kept up,—& what an exhaustless & universal interest *all* the people have in them,—a bad sign taken in connection with some other things. The military of Savannah have a large parade ground & here thousands of people were gathered.—I noticed at once the superior look of these Georgians to any other Southern people I had seen (—& have seen since.) They looked more like N.Y. people in energy & life,—tho' there was a plenty of long hair, & shambling even among them,—but not among the troops & their immediate friends.—*They* were about as fine, handsome & soldierly a set of men as I ever saw.—*The crème-a-la-crème* of the city, many of them old Confederate soldiers & officers.—The officer who drilled them,—Col Olmstead was one of the fiercest of their Georgia officers, & fought amongst other places at the fight just out of the city.[10]—(By the by it was near this same city thee may remember that Pułaski fell & there is in the city a very beautiful shaft to his memory.)[11] He was evidently an immense favorite,—& walking about in the crowd, almost adored one could plainly see, was Gen. Jo. E. Johnston. He is of medium height, somewhat broad as to shoulders & firmly built,—with very dark hair & whiskers, now turning grey, intensely bright & rather nervous looking eyes,—a moustache cut square, giving a harsh look to his mouth, somewhat pug as to nose, & fresh colored of complexion,—on the whole looking far more like a Northern than a Southern man,—& plainly full of energy.—To my mind he was by far the ablest general the South had,—but I looked away from him with a sick horror, when I remembered that under his command—with the almost absolute authority he possessed,—Salisbury & Andersonville poisoned the very air.

Almost all the militia companies here, as elsewhere through the South, wear a grey uniform,—picked out with various colors,—but the Col wore the regular Confed uniform,—grey with black velvet on the collar & black velvet trimmings,—a very handsome,—& very *ill suggesting* uniform.

Of course I noticed the absolute absence of the U. S. flag.—Save over one or two gov. buildings (U. S. Gov.) over the garrisons here & there, & over the National Cemeteries in which lie our dead soldiers the stars & stripes floats *nowhere* in the South.—It is as *foreign* a flag as it could be in China, & hated here, when it is at least respected there.

There stands on the parade ground a great, ungainly monument to the Confederate dead,—of grey stone or granite, with open niches in which stand two figures,—Sleep & Immortality of marble,—the white of the marble looking hideously incongruous in the midst of the grey of the stone.—It is like their taste, however, which is just about as cultivated as that of Choctaw Indians.

This slip is a specimen of the way the Savannah & other papers talked about me before I came,—afterwards when they found I was coming there & they were to have some adv. bills they were polite, & when I spoke, & the editors saw that all their "leaders" were there, & that they stood on their heads,—these grew very enthusiastic.

I had about 200 people to hear me in a very old, very quaint, very clean little theatre,—all the leaders in the town,—nine Confederate Generals among the number,—of these Jo. Johnston,—& Mr. Charles Green, an Englishman, the richest man in Savannah, & such a furious secesh, that when Gen Sherman came in, casting about for headquarters, he thought this man might as well suffer a little, & took possession of his elegant house.

They nearly took me by storm, after the lecture,—& the next day they literally over ran me, & were determined to take me to their houses,—where I went not.—It was partly that they really *did* admire me,—& partly that—as Col. Green said to Bernard—"they had discovered what a power that eloquence *must* be on the North the Northern side,"—& as *I* said, wished to placate it,—*I* was to be treated in such a manner as to make me think everything "lovely"—& to see & hear nothing save what they wished me to see & hear.—I would do nothing of the kind.—Tho' to be sure as I saw what they thought of me & considered my empty benches everywhere in the South—& remembered how my old Republican followers regard me & treat me. I could not help thinking, with a little bitterness that the appreciation—& hatred of my old enemies is far more enduring than the friendship—or gratitude of my old friends.

All the same I would not do what they wanted me to do.—Instead of taking their treatment of me—a passer by,—for a day as rule to judge by, I read their papers, a multitude filled with all bitterness towards the North & the negro.—I talked with divers & sundry Northern people who are here to *live,*—have lived here for years, & learned that if the mould of the church yard covered them proper could not shrink away from them more.—I thought it just as well too, when they thought I would be overwhelmed by *their* magnanimity & condescension towards a Northern woman—for the northern woman to go her way unheeding.—Also I did not propose to eat salt & break bread with them in their own homes & then go away & fall foul of them.—If I ever *have* anything to say about them, I want to say it with a clear way behind & before me.

I was amused at their arrogance & readiness to take offence, & old slave drivers ways,—& at the same time faculty of "subsiding" when they are properly met, by some thing that occurred while some of these ladies were calling on me.—I incidentally mentioned, in talking of Richmond, that while there "I had seen Valentine's statue of Lee."—saying Lee, just as I might have said Grant, or Washington, without any title,—& just now doubt as they had heard it said thousands of times,—but simply because I was I (though no doubt *I* have said *Gen* Lee in hundreds of instances)—they thought it was a purposed omission, & were determined to make me supply the gap.—

"You mean *Gen* Lee." said one of the ladies,—the wife of a rebel General (Lawton.)

I looked at her, & said,—"No,—I do not."

They all looked at one another in bewilderment,—"You,—You don't mean *Gen* Lee?"

"No, madame," said I composedly, "I mean Lee.—Robert E. Lee.—*Lieut Col.* Lee. I know of no legitimate legal authority to make him more than that." (thee will remember his rank in the U.S. Army was Lieut Col.)—& the ladies, finding I could fight, as well as they, quietly allowed the subject of conversation to be changed.

I heard a very queer sermon Sunday afternoon from a colored divine,—a funeral discourse of a girl who had gone from Savannah to Brooklyn & while at service there had taken fire & been burned to death,—& the [burthren?] of the preacher's discourse was, that she was very disobedient in going to Brooklyn, since her mother & friends wanted her to stay in Savannah (tho' it seems she was a bright, industrious girl & went away because she could do better)—& *that* was why she was burned to death, & over & all they were to take warning.[12]—He talked with the "mammy" of the girl & her brother sitting in front of him, & it seemed to them a very comforting discourse—& a very edifying one to the old "mammies" who sat about in their turbans & groaned.

You see these turbans now, on none save those who were pretty old, as slaves.—The younger ones hate them as a badge of servitude.—In the old times they *had* to wear these or go bareheaded,—they were not allowed to wear hat or bonnet,—&, if a slave met a white person, on the sidewalk, the slave had to step out into the street,—what a change it must be to all.

Now they are like peacocks as to finery,—such as it is.—They generally tho' looked very neat, as well as very fine on Sunday.

In the evening there was a discourse from a blind man, who somewhere had got hold of some sort of an account of Paradise Lost, & worked it up, in *his* style as the sermon,—& a hideous passage it was.—The people, generally, behaved themselves pretty well under his honors, but some of them proceeded to scream, & jump up & down like dancing jacks, & finally get stretched out stiff as tho' they were dead,—they had the "power" possess them.

No congregational singing, save while the choir "gave its money."—Here as every where, they have a spindling melodion, & a little thin choir, tooting & screeching away at regular hymns while the whole throng looks on in admiring silence,—or if it does sing, instead of singing its old fashioned melodies that all know, it sings "white folks hymns"—long [metre?], that the preacher "lines" to them.

About the money.—When the collection is taken up—they send round no hats,—would get nothing that way.—The preacher begs, & scolds, & argues with & exhorts them to give,—the stewards sit at the table down in the altar, & the people string out from their seats, & go up & put down their contributions on the table,—It is very funny. & when one does not give as much as the preacher thinks he or she ought, he proceeds to skewer them with some "fine irony"—& this being through,—the choir singing at intervals,—the turn of the choir itself comes, while the *people* sing & look on.

This particular collection was for moving the minister's furniture,—"$16 ladies & gentlemen,"—You hear very little of "brudders" & "sisters"—they are, even in church "ladies & gentlemen."

The church in which all this was done is the largest & best of the Savannah churches (colored)—& is ornamented in peculiar style,—The sun, the moon, & stars being painted round the face of the gallery, & overhead, on the ceiling a fearful & wonderful display of scenes from the bible,—The seven downward steps of the Prodigal, & the seven upward ones.—The Prodigal in this case being a good looking young darkey, dressed in the height of the fashion, his tempter being another good looking young darkey in a pea-green gown over enormous hoops,—& the very next picture being a spread eagle angel, very stout & strong, in an indigo colored gown.

I forgot to tell thee that Sat. evening I wandered & prowled through the markets for an hour & more talking with the people.—The market is very large & handsome, & Saturday evening is the great market for the most of the poor, & the colored folks.—Two thirds, I should say of the stalls are hired by colored people—many of them renting for from $150 to $170 a year. Butchers included.—Some of these people were exceedingly bright, & evidently able, one, who was a butcher's assistant when he was a slave told me he earned fully three thousand a year. The most of them were very kind & communicative, & were glad to be talked with, but there were a few *very* surly almost dangerous one would think.—& these I noticed as I have noticed in other similar cases, were *dead* blacks.—not the oily, shiny blacks, but those whose skin looks like blacking just put on & unpolished,—& Mrs. [Clives], one of the Northern ladies here, told me she had noticed the same thing.—The people who interested me the most were those old aunties & uncles who sat at the little stalls *outside,* the market, with their live chickens & little country "fixens,"—& who had almost all of the old simplicity of slavery. Mrs. [Clives] told me some [truly] interesting things about her life in N.C.—She went there with her husband at just the close of the war, when the "old" state of things had changed very little.

The place her husband bought had belonged to one of the largest planters in the state, & the "people" still staid on it & were hired by Mr. [Clives].

The next place was owned by another large planter in whose house was a state of things, common enough, it seems, *here,* but certainly curious to Northern observation.

The man who had owned *their* place had married some time before, & his wife brought to her new home a number of slaves, amongst others a quadroon, her maid, with whom the husband presently fell violently in love, & the maid with him.[13]—The wife made a row, & tried on divers occasions to induce her husband to sell the girl, but failed.—After some years, he being absent from home, she sold the *girl's child* to a Southern trader, & the girl herself to this *next* neighbor, who wanted her, & had long been known to want her for his own purposes.—Which altogether was a devilish piece of work for *even* a Southern *woman.*

When the husband came home there was an awful row, but the thing couldn't be undone,—by the state law, she could sell her *slave* property, if her *father* ratified the deed (tho' she could bear no control over her property in any other way)—which she had been careful to have done,—& tho' her husband offered five times the amount for which the girl had been sold, it was refused.

She really loved him, & wanted to be true to him, & tried to be.—Her new master wished her to give herself to him willingly,—& because she refused he had her strung up & lashed again & again,—the last time till the blood ran down in a little puddle into her shoes, & she fainted away.—After that she gave in,—had four or five children by him,—these children & their mother living in the same house as the wife & her children, on the whole having an even better time, & the best sort of feeling prevailing all round,—& they were still & *are* still living so all these years after the war.

And yet, so anomalous is the state of things here,—when our army passed this place, one of the officers halted at the door & politely asked of the mistress a glass of water,—she, hating the "Yankees" beyond measure called this woman & told her to carry a glass of water on a tray, which was done.—the officer drank the water, put down the glass, thanked her, the mistress, as he raised his hat,—when she cried out—"Don't thank me,—I wish it might choke you.—Why don't you put your arms around your *sister* then & kiss *her!*—that's what you came here for."

It so happened the officer had heard of the case from some of the negroes,—& again raising his hat answered blandly—"I am not yet sufficiently Southern for that Madame,—but—if I *had* to kiss either I would decidedly prefer your husband's *mistress* to his wife."—In which I rather think he *had* her.—The idea of these creatures talking of the *Northern* people being unduly fond of the negro.—As one of my chambermaids, a bright mulatto said to me "Civil Rights! We've had more of civil rights, & yellow niggers dan *we* wants for *shore*[.]"[14]

I was amused & disgusted too over something that happened in connection with my second lecture, in which I had a great deal to say about compulsory education, as it applied to the ends of their own section. Being through *all* of the editors, with divers more, thanked me for the speech, said how much it was needed & how timely it was.—Then when I saw the next days papers, I found not a word of *report* of what I had said, but a flattering notice of my "grace & eloquence" & the assertion that the "speech would be an admirable one for the North, but did not at all apply to the condition of things in *our* section."—Which is a specimen of the way those who *know* better, in this "section" steadily mislead, & keep in the dark their readers.—Georgia "not need it"! When the entire amount of money she has spent on *all sorts* of schools, black or white, & for school purposes of all sorts has been only about $600,000 in considerably over two years,—& the great body of the negro & poor white children do not go to school at all!

I went back to Charleston as I had come, only in a driving storm, & was called upon in the evening by Mr. Worthington the collector of the Port, who fairly *entertained* me by his detestation of these people & their doings.[15]—"Why wasn't Charleston utterly destroyed by the bombardment?" cried he.—"there were a thousand reasons why it *should* have burned down from the shelling, not one why it should have escaped,—& yet a thousand dollars would repair all the damage done to the *great* business houses.—*Why* was it?!—I'll tell you why!—Because the Almighty is reserving it for a worse fate!—And why, when the tidal wave came up here seventy feet did it stop short of swamping that Battery & all its fine houses?—Why,—I'll tell you why,—the rich people who live in them would have had time to escape from them.—They could run away from the fire,—They could run away from the water,—*I-tell-you,* the Lord has got *something* in store for them from which they *can't* run away,—& I want to be there to see it!"

In the cars going back to Columbia I noticed a man puzzling & puzzling over a notice which is very common here.—"Gentlemen will not put their feet on the seats nor spit upon the floors,—others must not,"—& after firing a perfect *salute* all about it, he gave it up & got off at some little station.

I think I have told thee of how the Dem Editor, & the leading secesh element in the town had howled over me, & promised me a crammed house, if I came back.—Well! Bernard is never really cast down, but he put in an appearance late in the afternoon, & informed me I would have *no* audience at all,—except the Dem editor aforesaid & one or two of *his* friends, with a few colored people—which proved to be the exact truth.—The editor, & the hotel keeper & divers others saw Bernard, & informed him, that the conductor of whom I before told thee, had reported my enormities, in talking in friendly wise with Henry Purvis, & that the town was *outraged.*—"They say she let him buy & pay for her ticket to Charleston" (which, it is needless to say was an absolute lie, even as to the *briefing,* B. looking as always after baggage & tickets) "& they talk about her *vilely.*"—The editor who was a man of sense, & knew how this would look—by my presentation elsewhere—did all he could in the way of *talk* to say how he felt about it, & came to hear me,—but he was careful not to say a solitary word in his *paper* to set his interesting readers right.—I had but *eleven* white people to hear me—they staying away *avowedly* because of this & this alone.—I confess I was edified, when the *next morning,* I read the report of Gov. Chamberlain's speech at Lexington, in which he set forth how "lovely" every [*sic*] was & is here,—& of what fraternal sentiments are growing up in South Carolina.

I had a very pleasant visit of a day with Mrs. Chamberlain & her mother & was more than amused by hearing their old darkies talk.—They had all been slaves on the place & have lived with the C's since they took it,—& are all very proud of belonging to the *Governor's* family.

One, the Coachman,—Washington by name,—black as ebony, with a funny little white fringe *all* round his face, was a study.—While we were out riding Mrs. C told him of something some Northern correspondent, who had been there a week before, had said about the Gov's equipage.—It is a very unpretending little phaeton with one horse,—but all the dignities of the law surround it, in Washington's eyes,—& his wrath was great when he was informed that this profane scribbler had asserted that the whole turn out was not worth more than $300.—

"Not worf more'n free hunder dollars!—" cried he, irate.—"I would just like dat man to know Lou (Louis the horse) ain't for sale,—an de *Gov'nor* aint for sale, an *I* aint for sale."—& with a flourish of his whip he drove on in dignified silence.

A little while after we came back, he was doing something to the plants—no one else being visible—on the front piazza, when a party of Northern tourists drove past in an open barouche & stopped to look at what they had evidently been told was the Governor's mansion.

Seeing this sedate looking darkey they hailed him, & asked "who lives here."

"*I* lives here"—answered Washington.

"*You?*"

"Yes, *I* lives here—me 'n my folks."

A consultation of wonder—evidently they thought this was one of the "stealing state darkies" living in style,—for one of the party at last said—"Oh—I thought Gov. Chamberlain lived here."

"De gubner?—You're right dere for *shore* Miss De gubner an his folks, dey lives here wid *me.*"—& the party drove on wiser than when they came.

I saw on Saturday afternoon going from Columbia to Augusta essentially what I had seen before in the way of "scenery" & was edified to hear one interesting son of the soil, holding forth to a Northern man on the train, about what a pleasant ride it was, & a beautiful country, & how it didn't make one tired to travel when one had such a pleasing "variety" to look at.

This same interesting gentleman—one of the magnates of Augusta, as I afterwards learned,—hearing me say something to the conductor about a telegram, (I was asking about a sleeping car, but the man before me had no idea *what* I was talking about) coolly turned round,—& said "telegram?—telegram?—what are you going to send a *telegram* about."

—"My own business"—said I,—at which he looked as if he would like to stick a knife into me.—They are ignorant, impudent, & boorish,—but if you act with even common self respect towards them, they are instantly "a proud, chivalrous & sensitive people that brook no insults."—

Oh!———

At Augusta I got a sleeping car for Macon.—B had gone on to Atlanta to look after business there, & I was going to Macon to see Andersonville on Sunday,—Andersonville lying sixty or seventy miles below there.—

And the sleeping car was a curiosity!—It was a regular *day* car, but with the reverse seat turned over & *locked* half way down so as to make a very much longer space than if it were shut down close,—slats put across, under the cushions, & a mattress put on top,—some sort of little hooks on the ceiling from which thin & shabby little curtains descended.—Of course nothing was *above* you,—& the shabby curtains were far better for comfort,—since they let in so much more *air,* than the heavy drapery of the Pullman cars.—The road tho' was frightful, & I lay awake listening to the talk of a couple of Virginians, a Georgian & the conductor.—No one else was in the cars & they thought

I was sound asleep,—or probably thought nothing about me,—for they knew nothing about me,—& so I heard the discourse, unobstructed of some well informed Southern men.—The one was a tobacco manufacturer,—the other Virginian, an old gentleman, was seemingly a being of "elegant leisure[″] from Lynchburg,—the Ga was a merchant, & the conductor, was as are almost all the conductors hereabouts, the scion of a house "ruined by the war."

They *did* spread themselves.—Their hatred of the Government, their howls over the past, their frantic eagerness for the election of a Dem. President when all their slave property will be paid for, would I think have converted even a Copperhead, who loves his money—to Republicanism.

They all *expect,* & not merely hope, to get paid for their slaves if the Democratic party gets into power once more,—&, if they don't get it, which they certainly won't, it will nevertheless make such a wrong stir & commotion here, that for the sake of the real good of the South, quite as much as for that of the North, it is to be hoped, a Republican President—on a regenerated republican platform, will continue to administer the Gov.—till this generation, at least, has passed away.—

At Macon I met those pleasant people, Mr. & Mrs. [Clives], who used to live at Macon, & who had come over to go to Andersonville with me.—

A leading man in the place, who knew them, & had always slighted them, seeing us together at breakfast, straightway came over to our table, & tried to join himself to the party,—of course *I* did not know *who* he was,—supposed he was a friend of theirs & was civil to him accordingly.—After we left the hotel, & were in the car, *he* appeared,—Mr. [Clives] by & by came to me & said—"Mr. Browne is very anxious to go with us.—You have been so praised by all the Savannah papers he thinks it will be a great thing to talk about afterwards,—that's the long & the short of *that* matter."

"What did you say to him?" asked I.

"I told him, that you were going to see the graves of martyred Union soldiers, & that it was a certain fact you would want no such person as him along.—That if he chose to go to Andersonville, on that day, on that train, there was no law to forbid it, but that I knew *you* wouldn't want him with you."

In spite of which he came along,—planted himself directly behind us, & tried to get into conversation, but I absolutely would not speak to him, till at last he went away to some other people.

The Conductor seemed exercised about our going to Andersonville (they have changed the name to *Anderson*) & proceeded to inform me of how *well* our men were treated, & of how much the people of the country did for them.—They had actually, at one time, of their own accord,—sent the men ten *barrels of vinegar.*—& at another time, when there was *no* food there, down below them car loads of meal were waiting to be brought up, & tho' his engine was limping, & it was not his business to drag up freight, he had actually brought this meal from Albany to Anderson.

Also he informed me, in unconscious fashion that "this road was as bad almost, as a battle to the Federals.—Scarce a train went down without an accident (the prisoners always went on special trains) & a good many killed."—An accident!—After all, it was a mercy beyond calculation that saved *any* of these men, by *any* means, from the fate that was before them.

All over this country they lie without stint about this whole thing.—They assert that far more of *their* men died with us, than of ours with them.—That none of them were starved,—That they *were* starved because they were too poor to feed them, & *our* Gov would neither exchange nor send them provisions,—& the vile, infamous Copperhead Northern papers are helping them on with all these lies.—They are at least getting to the point, not when they are at all ashamed *themselves,* of what they did, but when they can see the world's opinion of it, & try to shift the responsibility,—the *leaders* I mean,—the people seem to be satisfied with the thing as it stands.

I asked every Georgian I saw about the land & the crops (it is the richest part of the state hereabouts) in the *present,* so as not to put them on their guard,—& then inquired about the same section during the war,—& was told in every case, that the crops were abundant, & the *people* had no stint of anything.

When we reached the crossing just before getting to Andersonville, we were let off the train, & went our way to the Cemetery.

[Here Dickinson included a line drawing showing the railroad tracks, the station, the prison, and the cemetery.]

We went up the road from the crossing to the Cemetery which is just about in its original shape,—not yet *walled* in.—The *whole* ground being fenced about.

Even here, with the frightful witness of these graves against them, this Browne, who had reappeared began talking to Mr. [Clives] about *their* men being treated worse than ours,—that hundreds of them, thousands of them had been stained, but not one Yankee.—

I nearly strangled, I couldn't speak to him, but I beckoned to the colored man, the Supt's assistant *who* was with us, & said,—"my friend come & walk between me & that man,—Don't let me *see* him, let us walk away quick so that we cannot *hear* him."—& at last, with that, the wretch had the decency to walk away.

The fence surrounds about 48 acres,—there are four

acres with the lodge & out buildings & about 80 acres all around the Cem with the right of way,—that is the property of the Gov.—Stretching across one end of this,—with a wide break of roadway & some other open space between (making *two groups of* trenches) are *85* trenches, in which lie 12859 men who died in the hell near at hand.—

—In all the ground there are 13717 buried here.—Including the Supt who died here a few years ago—six men who were hung on July 11 64, & 857—(371 known, 486 unknown) who have been brought from near battle grounds.

Away off in one corner lie 118 rebel soldiers who died while they were engaged in watching the tortures of our men.—I cannot bear to have them lie within the same enclosure,—not for the sake of the dead, but for the sake of the living.

The Supt who died here had, I believe *been* here (as a prisoner I mean),—&, as the colored man told us, he was carried out in his arms to sit under the flag when he was dying, & ordered his grave to be so made that the shadow of the flag or its staff should fall always over him.

The men who were hung lie in six graves quite by themselves,—They were desperate fellows who murdered some of their comrades to rob from them food & money with which they could have a chance to escape.—The prison authorities took no note,—they would have been only too glad for our men to have sunk to the line of beasts or fiends,—but in all that horror they were determined that order & manliness should prevail, & by our common consent the men were arrested, a court & jury convened.—the men allowed counsel,—regularly convicted, sentenced & hanged them,—& it was the last disorder, or meanness of any kind ever known in that awful pen.—

The men who have been since buried lie in separate

graves, & make the more marked a peculiarity of the trenches that at once strikes you.—The little head boards instead of standing so [3 line drawings of headstones appear here]—as they ordinarily do,—with a space between each one,—stand so [3 line drawings of headstones touching each other appear here] not a fingers width scarcely between, & you stop to think what it means.—The long shallow trenches—not 2 feet deep—hold the men without coffins & without space between, laid down side by side, touching one another, & the dirt so cast over them—of these 12859—12411 are *known* through the faithfulness of their comrades.—A list was kept, of each man as he died,—a little stick, marked 1, 2, 3, &c put up at each head, & this number kept with the name in the register,—& so when Clara Barton came here it was easy to find where the name should be placed.[16]

That *whole* Andersonville story is without likeness in the annals of time.

These nearly thirteen thousand men perished in less than 14 months.—The first death—just after the place was opened, was on Feb. 27. 64—the last April 25. 1865,—&, as I noticed, on a *single* day, that of Aug 20.64, *113* men died.—

I thought I felt all I could feel at these graves but the sight of the stockade, still standing, was an even more horrible one than the quiet mounds.—*There* it was completed.—*Here* it had been done.—The space covered by the prison—(I mean of course enclosed is 27 acres.) the high posts must stand 12 or 14 feet,—the sentries walk is outside, the dead line was inside. There is an outer stockade put up when they expected more men, but when the war put an end to their deviltry.

The posts,—(trunks of trees) stand a hand's breadth apart, so that those outside could constantly watch those inside.—There are a few old trees standing, & quite a growth of underbush, fresh sprung, & in this these rotting, grey, ghastly looking pillars stand forth. The soil is red clay,—grass there was none in the prison days,—shelter there was absolutely none, for the scorching heats of summer, & the storms of autumn & winter, with fresh growth all about them.—Just *outside* the dead line a pretty stream runs by a constant temptation to death, *inside* are only *wells* of water.

A man at the station, an old guard here, told me in a perfectly frank way, as an incident he thought might please & interest me, that "they" (the guard) used often to drop bits of food *just* outside the dead line, so they could pick off a Yank as he reached out for it."

On these 27 acres, at *one* time 32,000 men have been crowded,—more than a thousand men to an acre.

One colored man lived all his life, but a few miles from here,—& has lived *here* ever since the war.—"Had he ever been here during the war?"—["]No, a great many of the colored people had tried to help the soldiers, & got strapped for it, & did no good, & if he couldn't *help* them, he couldn't bear to come & see such sights as he heard of here."

"Did any of the white people try to help them."

"A few who were Union folks,—I, with my own eyes, saw an old gentleman stripped & *strapped* till the blood came for taking them food."

"Was there plenty in the neighborhood."

"Full plenty."

"Were the people sorry for them."—

"No indeed. They used to be glad of it, because it disabled so many *Yankee* soldiers."

There is no need to ask questions. The place bears its silent but trumpet tongued witness against all this

South.—Let it be known forever, till they learn to have at least some shame for the honor of their deeds.

The little county of Colquitt, south of Andersonville, held a body of outlawed, persecuted Union people, who, in spite of their own sufferings, made the desperate effort to help these men at Andersonville to escape.—A party of 25 penetrated *almost* to the prison gate, but could get no farther, some were shot, some escaped.

The prison gate is but a short distance from the station, & I wondered with tortured wonder, what men—who got fresh from the cars, still full of life & energy—must have felt & suffered, as they came among this army of starving comrades, & saw *their* fate in these comrades forms & faces.

It was a terrible day, & yet a day I would not count out of my calendar on any reason.

I went my way back to Macon,—which is a fair looking place, spite of its rough streets,—& we all went to a darkey church in the evening where we heard some *old fashioned* singing. The preacher preached from Revelations, & a very funny sermon it was.—

But I must tell thee about it tomorrow.—I had thought to have finished my Southern experiences today—to day is *now* the 2 of May, but if this is to go off on the mail, I must close abruptly.

I hope my dearest Marmee is having a good, & pleasant time in Phila, & that she is well,—& I send her my heart.

Anna

Marmee,

This is the 3rd long letter I have forwarded.—I hope all have come safely.

Evansville, Indiana

5.3.1875

Dearest Marmee,—I remembered, after scrawling from Nashville, that I did mean to tell thee about the "Hermitage" at Savannah.—It is one of the largest of the old rice plantations,—4000 acres,—& is still in the hands of the family that owned it for generations "before Sherman"—McAlpine,—a scotch family originally.[1]

It must have once been a very "fine" place, as they call places here fine.—The house stands a good mile back from the road, the avenue to it having an irregular, but handsome growth of live oaks, & plenty of flowers.—It,—the house—faces the river,—front & back alike,—but a story & a half high, with wide verandah about it,—up the front, at the end of the avenue nearest the house—or rather up the back—if there is any choice between front & back—the one facing on the river, the other on the avenue, are the negro quarters. Standing on either side are scores & scores of cabins, little square places, with an unglazed window, & a huge outside chimney & earthen or brick floors,—very comfortable they were considered for slaves, but the few people, who work there now, have other abiding places.—These, tho' are left on their original estate.

In driving to it we went out of the *old* part of Savannah,—& meandered all round & round to see it,—the part originally settled by Oglethorpe,—Yamacraw by name.[2]—The streets are as narrow as allies [*sic*], wholly unpaved, & without drainage, the houses crowded, & battered, tho' some of them are picturesque in spite of their smallness & age, by *reason* of their age & quaintness.—Here pretty much all of the rows & desperate doings of Savannah originate, & here the scamps take refuge, & here the yellow fever *always* begins & rages.—Why in the world *even* Southern people do not make *some* move to change it, is a mystery to the Northern mind.

There is a good story about this place in connection with the last election.—The Republican candidate,—who was a Northern man—had said *his* say,—& it had been a pretty damaging one about the other man's "record"—when *he* got the floor he "sloshed" round about his "family" & his "name" & his place & work & history & pedigree,—& announced that no Northern man, no stranger, nor Yankee need come there to try to prejudice *these* people against him. *They* knew him, he & his had lived there for generations. *They* were no carpet baggers but belonged to the place from its beginnings. *His* ancestors had come over with the *first* ship load, that braved this wilderness, & settled here with Oglethorpe at Yamacraw.

Whereupon the Northern man announced,—being better informed, historically, than his neighbor,—that he was glad his neighbor aforesaid, had no false pride,—& that a man was *not* responsible for his ancestors, & that one might be better than the stock from which he come,—still he *must* confess himself somewhat surprised at the readiness of his friend to confess to his direct line being a descent from this first ship load of settlers, at Yamacraw, seeing that the first ship load was one of *transported convicts.*—He rather had him.

Also I did mean to tell thee of how while I was at Andersonville, & stood near the gate, I remembered with thrilling clearness a story that was told me years ago, about this very place,—& wondered whether, perchance as I walked to & fro I stood on the very spot to which the little boy crawled.

Years ago, near the close of the war, I was at some little town in Central New York, & in the course of my speech told a story of Andersonville.—There sat near me a plain, pleasant looking farmer & his wife, who seemed most wonderfully interested & moved by what I was saying.—The speech being done they came & talked with me for a while in the ante-room, & told me their story.

The father was lame & could not go to the war.—So eager was he, that having been twice refused as a volunteer, & knowing they "wan't so particular" about drafted men,—tried to go as a substitute, but was too disabled even for that.—That [*sic*] had married late,—had but one child, & he a little boy.—No grown up son to fight for flag & country,—&, it was a great sorrow to them that they & theirs could do nothing for a cause so dear to them, in its need.

By & by the little chap grew restive,—he was his parents own child, he was then years older than when the war began, nearly thirteen, & he begged & prayed to be allowed to go as a drummer boy,—till at last they consented.

And so, as they went on to tell her, he marched, & he played, & on more than one battle field got a rifle in his hand in place of his sticks, & fought as became a brave soldier, & was an enormous pet & favorite with his men.

One day he was taken prisoner & was marched away to this hideous hell of Andersonville.

Thee will remember that the temptation was constantly offered our poor perishing fellows that if they would take the oath to the Confederacy, they could go out free, & now & then, at rare intervals a man gave way under the intolerable strain & went out.

So, as a comrade afterwards told his father & mother, their boy, too weak to walk, or to stand, crawled one day towards the gate, outside of which was life, & plenty & dishonor,—& one of his perishing friends, lying near, drew out of his tattered uniform a scrap of a battle torn flag, & holding it in the palm of his hand turned it, with no words, towards the eyes of the dying boy.

—It was enough.—He crawled towards it, got it in *his* hands, kissed it, cried over it, prayed over it, & dragged himself back to his few more days of martyrdom,—&, as the comrade, who brought the word,—he who had seen it all, & helped by all he had,—his sympathy & love, in this sore hour of need,—told them, when the little fellow was dying in his arms, he kissed him, & then again, & again—& said "That is for father. That is for mother. Carry them my love, & my good [. . .] & tell them, that I'd rather have died for the dear old flag,—in battle,—but, as her honor needs it, I'm willing to *starve* for it here.—& I want them to be willing to.—

"And so," as father & mother said, with broken hearted pride, "he starved—& died."—

Let me get away from it—I will go back to our darkey meeting & tell thee about the absurd sermon.—We perched ourselves out on the steps to hear the singing, & one old brother & another came to look after us, & to insist, in hospitable wise on our going in, till in an ill starred moment we yielded & went.

Straightway yr preacher beheld a small row of "de white folks," he spread himself & went in. He didn't have such an opportunity every day, & he proposed to make the most of it.—He informed his congregation speedily that he was "gwin too preach de *gospil, an* to tell de trufe to folks ob all colors *white* an *black,* an all de shades between."

Well! as I told thee it was from Revelations he preached,—"And he had a pair of scales in his hand."

He told us about how "de Lord had casted away John on de Island of Paramos"—but finally concluded to amend *that* statement, & after giving us some information about the size & productions of the aforesaid island, announced that "de outlaws, yes bruthers an sisters de outlaws (*what* outlaws he revealed not) an de robbers, an de murderers, an dose men whose lot is to be in de lake of fire an brimstone forever, bound him, an robbed him, an casted him away on de Island of Paramos."[3]—"An bruthus an sisters—he had a pair of *scales* in his hand."

So he went on about John, about Christ, who, he told us, had been born in a "barn," & had turned the water to wine at Cana when he was about thirteen years old, and about Paul & Silas, & about old man King (old man king as well as I could make out being some slave they had all known) and about everything known & unknown in the heavens above, or the earth beneath, or the hell he seemed to think was gapping for the most of us, & he would cry, & scream, & beat his breast, & sing song in a tremendous voice that could be heard a quarter mile away, & not a solitary sentence he said had any earthly connection with any other, and whenever he would be apparently *stuck,* & would need a bridge to help him over, he would cry with double fervor "an he had a pair of *scales* in his hand!"—I wish I could remember his description of what he expected to enjoy when he got to heaven,—amongst other delights he announced—"Den we will go roun an roun, an up an up,—& *plumes* will grow from our shoulders—oh yes, bredren an sisters, *plumes* will grow from our shoulders,—not little chicken down, but big as turkey wings, an fine as peacock feathers—*f—or—r—he* had a pair of *scales* in his hand."

He held forth for a mortal hour & we sat through it to hear their wild singing at the end.—They were nearly all *old* slaves & held to their old fashions,—& they sang some strange melancholy things—amongst them, as well as I could make out—this

"Why can't you do like Peter did,
  A walkin' on de sea,
He clapped his hands to his dyin' Lord,
  Oh, Good Lord, remember me,
Member de rich an member de poor,
Member de bond an de free;
An when You are done a membering round
  Dear, Good Lord, remember me.["][4]

From Macon to Atlanta the country is "as usual"—Tho' that day, the 26th the people were all out in holiday laziness,—looking, so far as the laziness was concerned very like everyday laziness,—still one could see it was a "close" holiday,—all they shops were shut, & all the people were celebrating the day "Memorial Day." At Atlanta, the entire place had emptied itself in the streets.—The morning of Memorial day is given to the making of wreathes &c.—After dinner they have the oration, then the procession to the Cemetery, the prayer, the decoration of the graves, the salute, & afterwards some sort of drill, or military display.

After dinner we went over to the opera house, which was crowded, to hear the oration of Captain Henry Jackson,—& failed to be *edified.*[5]—The crowd was a frowsy, ignorant looking crowd, as all Southern gathering are,—to begin with,—& it *stank.*—Soap & water are not things, here, in demand.

The band played divers airs to which no heed seemed to be given till it suddenly struck up the "Bonny Blue Flag" (one of their famous rebel airs) when the crowd literally yelled,—& yelled still louder, when this was followed by "Dixie."

The "oration" gave us some *information* at least.—Amongst other things that the South *"chose"* to lay down its arms, "that its victorious legions were driving the ranks of its invaders before them, charging its artillery & capturing its guns *after* the fatal day of Ap—*po*—ma—tax" (as he called it,—& seemed to stick on it even at that) Also, "that while there might be those who called Gen. Robert E. Lee *traitor*, he was true to *every* principle ever held dear by God & humanity."

Also—"that when people in future ages sought for deeds of heroic valor, the 300 of Greece, & the old Guard at Waterloo, & the charge of the Light Brigade would be forgotten in the record of the splendid heroism of the Confederate Dead."

The whole speech was used, as all these speeches (I have read a great many in the "exchange") are used, & as the day itself is used, not really to do honor to the memory of the dead, but "to fire anew" the hearts of the living to hatred.—There is not one word nor effort spoken, nor made towards a "reconciliation."

Their real indifference to their dead struck me very strongly out at the Cemetery. There are a great many soldiers graves, & a monument to them,—& this near a city. Yet the graves were flat & uncared for, & the head boards in very ill repair.—The square in which these rested was marched around by the military—the circuit of it made to reach the monument.—A Northern soldier's grave is something held almost sacred,—yet these people there ostensibly for the sole purpose of paying respect to *these* broke over them, by thousands, trampling & dishonoring them, almost breaking down the head boards, in their eagerness, to get a sight of Gen Anderson, who was chief marshal of the day, & of his procession following.[6]

"They *are* more than half savage" I heard one intelligent looking U. S. soldier say to another, the two lookers on like ourselves.

I had some talk with these men, who had just come from special duty in Alabama "where," as one of them said "the people don't yet know the war is ended."

They told me of one case—of a Republican speaker, who, while he was on the platform had a message delivered him that his wife was dying (an arranged lie)—who sprang on to his horse to get speedily to his home, & at a lonely place was met by a body of men, & without warning, or a chance to defend himself, was *riddled* with their bullets, twenty seven shots being found in his dead body.

While we were talking, so that no one could hear what we were saying, it was curious to watch the suspicious glances that were cast on us, & how people walked & stood close to try to hear what we were saying.

—I had the best house tho' that I have had anywhere in the South,—& the people were genuinely enthusiastic about me & my speech.

Come the next day, the 27 to Chattanooga, reaching there at 4 in the afternoon. The country out of Atlanta is really beautiful, wild & mountainous,—& all the way to Chattanooga it is picturesque, & for the last 38 miles, from Dalton up, specially full of historic interest.—Almost every foot of the way having been hotly contested.

We did not see the field of Chickamagua,—[fated?] field to us, as it lies 7 miles back from the road,—but we swept along past Missionary Ridge, & in full sight of Lookout Mountain long before we came to Chattanooga.[7]

After Rosecrans lost us us [*sic*] Chickamagua, the army poured, a disorganized mass in towards Chattanooga which point our men held, & were stopped, as they came through a little gap in Mission Ridge by Gen Thomas & reformed into an army. A little to one side of this gap is the tree by which were Gen Bragg's head quarters, where our men drove all before them a few days afterwards,—& yet a really bright looking "native" standing on the platform of the car, announced to us that "*there* was Grants head-quarters, where the Confederate army under Gen Braxton Bragg *took* the heights.—"

To this day then there are people who, right then in the face of the most ignominious defeat the South suffered, really believe it was the "Yankees" that were whipped.

The Chattanooga papers, that had put up their noses at me, when they found I had actually been there, & been on the mountain, & gone my way, without talking in their dingy town relieved themselves after this fashion.—Which is thoroughly Southern.—They care nothing at all about you, insult you, or leave you entirely alone,—but if you simply go on *your* way without noticing them, they are straightway insulted.

Lookout Mt. is about 2200 ft high,—& I went up it, getting some beautiful outlooks in spite of the storm, through a driving rain.—Mrs. Rouble's Cottage to which I had been directed is about a mile back from the "point"—where the battle was fought,—& in the morning we went out there.—A photographer, who is there planted, an old U.S. soldier, pointing out the ground to us.

The mountain is about 80 miles long, running North & South,—its Northern *point* far higher than the rest of it—a basin all about it,—straight off to the east, lower, but running in an almost parallel line Mission Ridge.—And the outlook, far & wide, is over open rolling country, & far off ridge.

It is a spot to make a patriot proud.—The rebels held this mountain,—cannon planted on the very top,—a *natural* fortification that seemingly nothing could have overcome, & yet up its broad sides, up its steep face, up to the very mountain summit, the last ascent made by scaling ladders our men fought their way to victory,—fighting from 8 in the morning—when the[y] made their "fight above the clouds," till midnight.—& when the rebels retreated, they retreated to mission ridge, where they were again above us, & our men in the basin, under their fire, as *our* men said—"when they saw the boys in blue coming for them again they couldn't believe the evidence of their own eyes, & thought it was a [']dress parade.[']"—A dress parade that drove every thing before it.

I have "news" that will tell thee the whole story of the fight, when I get home.

In the afternoon, I went to the Cemetery,—a most lovely spot covering the entire of a little hill, of 75 acres, the graves rising in tiers,—& not set close together, with plenty of trees, & ornamental flowers & shrubs.

This Cemetery has, as they all have, the flag flying, & the upright cannon as a monument, & little scraps of poetry painted up here & there.—(I think none of these touched me as did one at Andersonville,—I had seen it often before but never *as* it shows *there,*

"Whether within the prison drear,
    Or in the battle's van;
The fittest place for man to die
    Is where he dies for man.")[8]

About 1/3 of the 78 acres is actually covered by graves.—Here from these hard fought fields, for sixty or seventy fields round about 12,931 men have been brought

7880 of them being "unknown." From the *field* of Chickamagua alone (not from its hospitals but in battle slain) there are 1638 men, unknown, in one place, & in another 812 graves that are filled by colored soldiers who fell that day.

From Chattanooga up to Nashville, the land looks better cultivated, & there is more show of industrious life, tho' as one of their leading rebel editors—Mr. [*Puries?*] of Nashville, said to me, the people there did not make out of 300 days more than what would be 100 *working* days in the North.

And their school fund tho' it is considered a model now, really provides for only about 4 month's schools in the year—unless the "county" sees fit to add to it,—& the "county," as a rule, doesn't see fit.

I heard one man ask another standing at the station where we got supper, "why he didn't get his fence up," (a great, hearty cur he was) & his reply that "when the old woman (meaning his wife) got through her spinning they'd take hold together & get it up.["]

And I had a good deal of edifying & unedifying discourse in the cars.—

The ride is beautifully mountainous for about 30 or 40 miles out of Chattanooga.—When we turn away from the Wild Country into the farming region of Middle Tennessee.

Nashville is a dirty, dusty, windy, dreary, dead looking city. Very few good shops, very few fine houses,—with the abundance of marble & stone all about, almost the entire of it built of dingy looking bricks.—The whole place has a stagnant & forbidding air.

The theatre was so filthy I was actually afraid of it,—& my dress looked as tho' it could *never* be made clean, from the stage, & the audience was wholly unlike any other audience I have had in the South save that of Wilmington—for I have had of the *best* every where, but this *best* was an ignorant, ill looking, common crowd, & not much of it.

The next day I drove about & walked about the place, & edified myself by reading the morning papers.—The notice in the "Union & American" is certainly the most absurd mass of contradictions I ever *did* see, & the silliest article for a "first class" paper.

The State house is the only fine building in the city.—Outside it are the new Fiske University buildings—really handsome as well as large, & the "Vanderbilt" as extensive building put up for some sort of school purposes, & presented by Com. Vanderbilt,—not yet finished.[9]

The State House is of very light stone, with high steps & imposing pillars all about it, the four sides being precisely alike, standing on higher ground, & with an extensive view of the hills & the Country round about.

Inside, in the stairways,—the finish of the rooms then is a great deal of Tennessee marble used—which is dark & handsome. The entire building is of native Tennessee material.

The furnishing of the Senate Chamber & Hall is very plain, even rough—splint bottomed chairs, & very common desks,—& the smell is musty & dirty.—There are no pictures, nor ornamentations of any kind.

The library is a curiosity [. . .] of bad daubs of pictures, some of them full length, & some of them big & some little,—& the most curious hodge podge as to the people, Parson Brownlow & Andy Johnson, Gen *Geo.* H. Thomas & Lee & Stonewall Jackson, & *Andrew* Jackson big & little & *Mrs* Andrew,—& Mr. Lincoln & Grant, & Jo Johnson, & about one hundred more.—The library looked not much to boast of, & the librarian, wonderful to tell is a *woman*—but she was not there.

The greater part of the building inside is built of something to hugely interest a geologist,—petrified things showing all over the face of the stone,—a fish here, a horse there, a man's face in another place, &c, as the Ethiopian brother who guided us announced bounding on to a table & flourishing a stick to show what he had to show, "all yus I will show you what you never afore seed in all de world de [nimbepress] of an helephant,"—& there, sure enough it *was.*

I stopped at the Fiske University, but they were not in session, & so I neither heard them "recite" nor "sing"—They have "sung" to good profit, have raised in that way about $100,000.

I was greatly pleased with *some* of the teachers with one a Miss Anna E. Alden from Athens Ga. especially. She was one of the persecuted unionists of the war, & is heart & soul in her present work.—They told me, that not a solitary lady from the city had ever called on them,—& I had reason to remember the city with love in connection with them.

Their music teacher, a graduate of Oberlin, & a very nice & ladylike looking young mulatto came to my first lecture with the rest of the teachers.[10]—When the usher saw her color he threw down the tickets & refused to seat *any* of the party,—they had to find their own places,—& there was a uproar all about them,—& a good many people announced they would not come to hear *me* again in consequence.

"In consequence" of this & of a far worse matter, I had almost *no* audience the next night.—An officer (police) had attempted to arrest a negro on the ground that he had been quarrelling with his wife (he was *not* quarrelling when the officer entered his house) & the negro drew his revolver on him, & the officer was shot dead.

The negro was arrested, & all the afternoon there was the wildest uproar through the place, thousands being gathered in the streets & about the jail. The whole place, Gov. Mayor, Sheriff, *everybody* knew the man was to be lynched, & not the slightest effort was made in *any* way to prevent it,—The riot-bell was rung about nine o'clock, only to call out a greater mob, & make a worse disorder, & the Mayor was actually walking about, as a citizen among the mobocrats.

The jailor was the only one who behaved like a man, in spite of all efforts & threats he refused to give up the keys, or to tell where they could be found, & the mob broke in *seven* doors to get at their victim,—dragged him out with a rope round his neck, ran him up the street, then men deliberately, one after another firing at him, & then flung him off the bridge 50 feet into the Cumberland below.[11]

The papers two days after realizing how this thing would sound elsewhere began to announce that the "well disposed citizens were dreadfully shocked"—& that the mob had consisted of very few people,—whereas the mob had not less than 10,000 people in it, & the whole city approved of the action. Bernard & I walked about the streets, & into the shops for hours the next day.—Nothing else was talked about, & everybody thought the thing "well done."

The man deserved hanging, no doubt,—but the whole barbarous proceeding against him, is a fair sample of the feeling here against the "niggers"—& of the respect, in any way, for "law & order."

My barber told me yesterday that thirty of the colored people had left the city since Thursday night,—& that a great many were leaving all the time,—they felt so "insecure" since the Democrats had got back into power.—"Where have they gone?" I asked.

"Dey are all congregating into Mississippi"—he answered—In which they are doing well.

I went to the Penitentiary & found there have about 1100 prisoners—only about 450 of them being in the prison,—the rest working out, in various parts of the state "on the road."[12]

The men in the prison are nearly all white, & are taught a trade.—They were making furniture of all sorts, & camphor wood boxes,—& the work shops, with the camphor wood smell were not unpleasant.—Also the cells of these whites were not such horrible places as some cells are. They were quite clean, & with decent beds, & a little spot of a place for artificial ventilation.—But the negro cells were horrible holes,—with wretched bunks, & no means of air save through the grated cell doors,—& the negroes themselves are taught no trade.—They are almost all "on the road"—or used as servants about the prison.

There is no library, & no chapel, & no books.—*None* of the convicts, scarcely, can read.

I saw a great many people at Nashville, of all shades of feeling, & they consciously & unconsciously gave me but one feeling, & that was expressed by Gen Pennypacker (who is a Pa boy, in command of our troops here) that "they are as big rebels as ever."[13]

And that reminds me of something I was going to tell thee about Lookout Mt.—There were at the point while we were there two boys, about 14 years of age, evidently "gentlemen's sons" & *very* nice looking,—dressed in the confederate grey uniform that marked them cadets of some military academy.—They were very restive while we were talking about the battle, & by & by they went up to some "relics" lying in the photographer's shop, & the one said to the other, "There's the gun stock of some G—D—Yankee, damn his soul."—

We were glad to get out of Dixie last night. Left Nashville at 3 in the afternoon, saw a bit of rather wild land for a few miles out, had an abrupt rise of Baker Hill,—the steepest grade I suppose, on an ordinary guage road in the U.S.—426 ft in a mile & nine tenths,—218 ft to the mile,—& after that ran through a wholly uninteresting country till long after dark we reached the Ohio river at Henderson, & struck another price of Southern enterprise. The city of Evansville has again & again tried to get the right of way to run down a road over the twelve miles to a spot opposite the city, where they will place a bridge, but the intelligent Ky legislature will not grant it. So the cars have to be run on to a transfer boat, & we 2 brought down these 12 miles *so,* consuming *two* hours in the transit.

As I said we were glad enough to get out of the South.—From a Southern point of view it had been an immense success,—the truth being, that B's mother-in-law paid the deficit of bills, there being a loss,—& save my travelling expenses of course I have not had a solitary cent,—&, as B says, & as all the editor's along the line say nobody else living would have done as well.

I have gained a good deal of information, for which I am glad, & now I must look for some money.—I am going to St Louis from here, & hope, next week, to send thee some money from there.

I have stood my journeying very well. The warm weather suiting me, & tho' I have been tired, I have not been *very* tired more than once or twice.[14]

I will be at St Louis over Sunday, at the Lindell House, & I want thee to let me have a line from thee there.

I think of thee always,—love thee always,—& send thee my heart.

Marmee.

Anna

When thee is done with the letters I have written to Julia to do them up in an express package & send them to Dickey.[15]—

Notes

Introduction

1. For a history of Dickinson's life, see J. Matthew Gallman, *America's Joan of Arc: The Life of Anna Elizabeth Dickinson* (New York: Oxford University Press, 2006). Dickinson's Southern tour is discussed on pages 136–41.

2. In postwar America, the "lyceum" essentially combined adult education with popular entertainment. During its heyday, popular orators traveled from town to town, delivering lectures on various topics to paying audiences. See Carl Bode, *The American Lyceum: Town Meeting of the Mind* (New York: Oxford University Press, 1956); Angela G. Ray, *The Lyceum and Public Culture in the Nineteenth-Century United States* (East Lansing: Michigan State University Press, 2005); Gallman, *America's Joan of Arc*, 63–79.

3. On the gendered responses to Dickinson's wartime oratory, see J. Matthew Gallman, "Anna Dickinson, America's Joan of Arc: Public Discourse and Gendered Rhetoric during the Civil War," in *American Public Life and the Historical Imagination*, ed. Wendy Gamber, Michael Grossberg, and Hendrik Hartog (Notre Dame, Ind.: University of Notre Dame Press, 2003).

4. *Cartes de visite* were small photographs, capable of cheap mass production.

5. The best overview of the period is still Eric Foner, *Reconstruction: America's Unfinished Revolution, 1863–1877* (New York: Harper & Row, 1988). For an excellent short history, see Michael W. Fitzgerald, *Splendid Failure: Postwar Reconstruction in the South* (Chicago: Ivan R. Dee, 2007).

6. On the economic consequences of emancipation, see Roger L. Ransom and Richard Sutch, *One Kind of Freedom: The Economic*

Consequences of Emancipation, 2d ed. (New York: Cambridge University Press, 2001).

7. For the African American experience during the transition from slavery to freedom, see Steven Hahn, *A Nation under Our Feet: Black Struggles in the Rural South from Slavery to the Great Migration* (Cambridge: Harvard University Press, 2003).

8. J. Matthew Gallman, "Is the War Ended? Anna Dickinson and the Election of 1872," in *The Memory of the Civil War in American Culture,* ed. Alice Fahs and Joan Waugh (Chapel Hill: University of North Carolina Press, 2004). On the Liberal Republicans, see Andrew L. Slap, *The Doom of Reconstruction: The Liberal Republicans in the Civil War Era* (New York: Fordham University Press, 2006).

9. See James M. McPherson, "Abolitionists and the Civil Rights Act of 1875," *Journal of American History* 52 (December 1965): 483–510. In 1883, the Supreme Court found the Civil Rights Act of 1875 unconstitutional.

10. It is not entirely clear how Dickinson and Bernard chose their itinerary, although it does appear that Bernard made the arrangements with the proprietors of particular lecture halls. Their route presumably balanced manageable travel distances with the likelihood of finding substantial and appreciative audiences. A more ambitious tour might have taken them as far south as Baton Rouge and New Orleans, but perhaps they concluded that the additional costs in time, money, and physical energy did not warrant adding Louisiana to their journey.

11. Anna E. Dickinson, *A Ragged Register (of People, Places, and Opinions)* (New York: Harper & Brothers, 1879).

12. If one reads these letters in the context of her other family correspondence, it becomes apparent that Dickinson envisioned them as the basis for future publication. Dickinson's letters home to her mother and sister were routinely full of amusing anecdotes and biting commentary about the people she encountered on the road, but these four long travel letters include more detailed observations about terrain and architecture and the larger social, political, and economic issues she encountered than her routine correspondence. At the same time, throughout these letters Dickinson often seemed to be writing to entertain her mother, rather than a larger audience. For the modern reader, it is probably best

to see these letters as observations in her authentic voice, unfiltered by concerns about audience and market. She probably wrote these four letters in pieces, sometimes catching up on events that had happened several days earlier, bringing letters to a close when it was convenient to mail a missive off to her mother. Had Dickinson opted to pursue a published book about her 1875 tour, she would no doubt have turned to these letters for observations and anecdotes, but perhaps we are fortunate to have her observations unfiltered by such considerations.

13. Harriet Martineau, *Society in America* (1837); Frederick Law Olmsted, *The Cotton Kingdom* (1861); Alexis de Tocqueville, *Democracy in America* (1862). Tocqueville published his celebrated analysis of American society in French in the 1830s.

14. Whitelaw Reid, *After the War: A Tour of the Southern States 1865–1866,* ed. C. Vann Woodward (New York: Harper, 1965). On postwar travel writings as a genre and Reid's rhetoric in particular, see Lori Robison, "Writing Reconstruction: Race and 'Visualist Ideology' in Whitelaw Reid's *After the War,*" *Journal of Narrative Theory* 29 (Winter 1999): 85–109.

In addition to Reid's *After the War,* see John Townsend Trowbridge, *The Desolate South, 1865–1866* (1866) and Sidney Andrews, *The South since the War* (1866). In 1865 the *Nation* sent columnist John Richard Dennett on an extended tour of the South, resulting in forty-two columns describing his observations. (All of these early postwar travel narratives have been republished in modern volumes.) A decade later, author Constance Fenimore Woolson published a series of essays on Reconstruction Florida. On Woolson, see Victoria Brehm, ed., *Constance Fenimore Woolson's Nineteenth Century* (Detroit: Wayne State University Press, 2001).

15. On Van Lew, see Elizabeth Varon, *Southern Lady, Yankee Spy: The True Story of Elizabeth Van Lew* (New York: Oxford University Press, 2003).

16. The scholarship on the Lost Cause and the memory of the Civil War is vast. For the crucial overview, see David Blight, *Race and Reunion: The Civil War in American Memory* (Cambridge: Belknap Press of Harvard University Press, 2001). For Confederate women and commemoration, see Caroline Janney, *Burying the Dead but Not*

the Past: Ladies' Memorial Associations and the Lost Cause (Chapel Hill: University of North Carolina Press, 2007).

17. Dickinson's observations about her hostile Southern hosts and her own continued distaste for the Confederate cause offer an interesting contrast to other evidence suggesting that by the middle of the 1870s many whites in both the North and the South had embraced a spirit of reconciliation. On postwar culture and reconciliation, see Nina Silber, *The Romance of Reunion: Northerners and the South, 1865–1890* (Chapel Hill: University of North Carolina Press, 1993).

Raleigh, North Carolina

1. Dickinson called her mother "Marmee."

2. Raised a Quaker, Dickinson customarily used "thee" in her letters to her mother.

3. Dickinson left a gap here where the arrival time ought to have been.

4. Reverend Thomas De Witt Talmage (1832–1902) was a well-known Northern pastor whose sermons were published in thousands of magazines and journals.

5. Dwight Lyman Moody (1837–1899) and Ira David Sankey (1840–1908) were celebrated evangelicals who wrote and performed religious music across the United States.

6. Here Dickinson is referring to commonly accepted "republican" virtues (such as the desire for independent and civic-minded citizens, and the rejection of corruption, inherited power), not the Republican Party.

7. In 1875 Ulysses S. Grant was in his second term as president of the United States. In 1872 Dickinson had campaigned for Grant's opponent, Horace Greeley.

8. Dickinson left a blank space where the number of miles would have been listed.

9. Dickinson routinely used the term "Ethiopians" to refer to African Americans.

10. Elmer Ellsworth (1837–1861) was killed while attempting to remove a Confederate flag flying at an Alexandria, Virginia, hotel that was visible from the White House, making him the first sol-

dier to die for the Union. Nathaniel Lyon (1818–1861) was the first union general and Theodore Winthrop (1828–1861) the first Union major to be killed during the Civil War. All three were considered among the war's first martyrs. The quoted passage is from "Watchers" by John Greenleaf Whittier (1862).

11. Often described as Gen. Robert E. Lee's greatest victory, the Chancellorsville campaign was fought between April 30 and May 6, 1863, in rural Virginia west of Fredericksburg. The following spring, the armies clashed on almost the same terrain at the Battle of the Wilderness.

12. Elizabeth Van Lew (1818–1900) was a staunch abolitionist; during the war she had supported the Union cause by working as a spy in Richmond. In 1875 she held a federal appointment as postmistress of Richmond.

O. W. Bernard ran the New York-based National Lecture Bureau. During the 1875 tour he served as Dickinson's agent and traveling companion. Bernard made all the travel arrangements and apparently often sold the tickets on the day of a lecture. On a few occasions during this trip the two split up, with Bernard going ahead to arrange events while Dickinson spent time touring.

13. In the Anna E. Dickinson Papers in the Library of Congress, these letters are filed under Dickinson's Family Papers, microfilm reel 3 (hereafter cited as AED Papers). But in those folders a large portion of this first letter is missing. The missing section, starting here and continuing on for about fourteen hundred words, can be found (unlabeled) among Dickinson's Miscellaneous Papers.

14. The Civil Rights Act of 1875 sought to end the exclusion of blacks from public places. Business owners who violated this bill were liable to substantial fines. Dickinson seemed to be concerned that the newly passed law would stir up racial antagonism in the South, making life for African Americans even more difficult. The Supreme Court found Congress's effort to regulate private companies unconstitutional and the act was overturned in 1883.

15. A passionate abolitionist, Senator Charles Sumner (1811–1874) was the first to introduce the bill that, after his death, would become the Civil Rights Act of 1875. Dickinson was a great admirer of Sumner and often sought his counsel earlier in her career.

16. This ends the section of this letter that is filed under miscellaneous letter fragments in the AED Papers.

17. Here Dickinson is mocking those Virginia elites known as the First Families of Virginia. The term "FFV" commonly referred to Virginians who could date their lineage to the colonial period.

18. Henry A. Wise (1806–1876) served as governor of Virginia (1856–1860).

19. Libby Prison and Belle Isle were notorious Confederate prisons in Richmond.

20. Edward Valentine (1838–1930) was a Richmond-born sculptor known for his creation of busts and monuments. Dickinson was particularly unhappy with his racist depiction of an African American boy in this famous piece of sculpture.

21. The Confederate White House was home to President Jefferson Davis and his family from 1861 until they evacuated the city in 1865. It served as military headquarters during Reconstruction, later became a public school, and today houses the Museum of the Confederacy.

22. Castle Thunder, like Libby Prison, was a tobacco warehouse before the war. When the city fell to Union forces in 1865, both were converted into Union prisons.

23. Hollywood Cemetery is the resting place of numerous Confederates: over eighteen thousand enlisted soldiers, twenty-five officers, and Jefferson Davis. Dickinson notes cavalry commander Maj. Gen. J. E. B. Stuart (1833–1864), who was killed at the Battle of Yellow Tavern, and Lt. Gen. Ambrose P. Hill (1825–1865), who was killed at Petersburg.

24. Hollywood Cemetery's soldier's monument is a ninety-foot pyramid erected in 1869 to pay tribute to the Confederate soldiers buried there.

25. The statue Dickinson describes is known as *Recumbent Lee.* Lee's widow selected Edward Valentine to create the statue, which depicts General Lee asleep in his tent after battle. It now resides, along with Lee's remains, at Washington and Lee University in Lexington, Virginia, as it has since 1883. Valentine finished the piece on April 1, 1875, making Dickinson among the first to see it.

26. Julia Gould was one of Dickinson's friends from New York.

27. The Richmond National Cemetery is about three miles east of the state capitol in Richmond.

28. Here Dickinson inserts a separate page with the notation: "From this point go to *14 ½* & *14 ½–2* to read,—*then* come back & *finish this* sheet, & go on to 15." This text reproduces the letter in the order Dickinson had intended.

29. This ends Dickinson's insert in the letter.

30. Throughout her career as a public speaker, Dickinson devoted much of her energy to lectures on contemporary events and reform topics. But audiences were often particularly pleased with her historic talk on the life of Joan of Arc, the famous French "Maid of Orleans." Audiences came to identify the fiery orator with her combative subject. For years on the lyceum circuit, Dickinson would pair her Joan of Arc lecture with a more political talk, delivering them on alternate days. During her 1875 tour, audiences seemed particularly anxious to hear her "Joan of Arc."

31. William Mahone (1826–1895) was a civil engineer, teacher, and prominent Virginia politician. During the war Major General Mahone was most known for his role in the Battle of the Crater during the Siege of Petersburg. The Crater (which Dickinson sometimes called "the Mine") was the product of an ingenious plan where Union soldiers tunneled under the short distance between the Union and Confederate trenches, laying explosives beneath the Confederate lines. The Union troops detonated the explosives on July 30, 1864, blowing a hole in the Confederate lines. The battle turned into a disaster for the Union, as troops charged into the crater created by the explosion and became easy targets for Confederate reinforcements. Mahone was credited with rallying the rebel troops and turning the tide. A few years after Dickinson's visit, Mahone would become a leader in Virginia's Readjuster Movement.

32. Dickinson commonly enclosed newspaper clippings in her letters. When she returned from tour, she would add these to her many scrapbooks.

33. Petersburg's Blanford Church was abandoned in 1806 and not restored until 1901.

34. Fort Sedgwick, nicknamed "Fort Hell," was an area of caves dug into the side of hills to protect Union soldiers from the intense bombing outside of Petersburg. Fort Mahone, named for William Mahone, was the Confederate stronghold called "Fort Damnation" by the soldiers who occupied the trenches.

35. Several regiments of U.S. Colored Troops participated in the Union charge at The Crater. Dickinson is referring to confirmed reports that Confederate troops fired upon surrounded black troops rather than letting them surrender.

36. John Dickinson, one of Dickinson's brothers, had accompanied her in her 1865 tour of the Fredericksburg battlefield.

37. On several stops on her tour Dickinson suspected that her hosts were trying to give her a positive impression of the South, thus "picking" appropriate audiences for her lectures.

38. Many white southerners felt that transplanted Northerners (carpetbaggers) and blacks were controlling the state legislatures.

39. Dickinson's letters are full of amusing anecdotes like this. On the one hand, she clearly grew tired of the constant interruptions when she was on the road, but on the other, she also enjoyed the attention and recognized that her profession depended on her fame.

40. This is in reference to the pantaloon-like garment popularized by Amelia Bloomer, and associated with radical women from the North. Although Dickinson apparently did not wear bloomers, she did create a bit of a stir when she donned trousers and rode horses astride while visiting the West.

41. Maj. Gen. Benjamin Franklin Butler (1818–1893) was in command of Fort Monroe, located in Hampton, Virginia. He is best remembered for refusing to return slaves who took refuge behind Union lines, claiming them as "contrabands" of war. Southerners also despised him for his infamous General Order No. 28, aimed at controlling the behavior of rebel women when he was commander of occupied New Orleans.

42. Nat Turner (1800–1831) led a bloody slave rebellion in Virginia in 1831.

43. A celebrated sculptor, Emma Stebbins (1815–1882) is best known for her *Angel of the Waters* in New York City's Central Park. After more than a decade of celebrity, much of that time spent on the road, Dickinson had at least a passing acquaintanceship with a long list of the nation's leading public women of the day, including artists, authors, actresses, and fellow lecturers.

Macon, Georgia

1. Postwar illiteracy was particularly high in North Carolina.

2. Landmark Communications owned the *Virginian-Pilot,* published in Norfolk.

3. The editor was speaking of the radical suffragist and activist Victoria Woodhull (1838–1927), who was notorious for her advocacy of "free love."

4. Bernard, who had shifted from the Democratic to the Republican Party, was suggesting that Northerners who visited the South would become strong Republicans dedicated to the continuing support of Reconstruction.

5. Dickinson appears to be using "smole" as the past tense of smile.

6. Dickinson and her traveling companion were joking about Harriet Beecher Stowe's *Uncle Tom's Cabin.* One of the book's most memorable characters was Tom's abusive master, Simon Legree, a transplanted northerner whose name came to represent greed and oppression.

7. Abolitionist minister Henry Ward Beecher (1813–1887) became the center of a huge scandal when abolitionist editor Theodore Tilton charged him with having an adulterous affair with Tilton's wife, Elizabeth Tilton. All three were among Dickinson's close friends. See Richard Wightman Fox, *Trials of Intimacy: Love and Loss in the Beecher-Tilton Scandal* (Chicago: University of Chicago Press, 1999).

8. Chain gangs were a punishment for criminals and a source of physical labor for the state. Black men were often disproportionately sentenced to the chain gangs after the abolition of slavery.

9. Apparently Dickinson is offering a phonetic spelling of "gaping" here.

10. Established in 1865, Raleigh's Shaw University is the oldest historically black college in the South.

11. Located in Andersonville, Georgia, Andersonville Prison was the largest Confederate prison and was notorious for the abusive treatment of Union prisoners. Salisbury Prison was in Salisbury, North Carolina, a short distance from Charlotte.

12. Dickinson is describing the Raleigh National Cemetery, established in 1865.

13. Confederate Memorial Day, often recognized on April 26, was a holiday commemorating fallen Confederate soldiers. Decoration Day, established shortly after the war, recognized the Union soldiers who died during the Civil War. After World War I, Decoration Day—renamed "Memorial Day"—became a day honoring the fallen in all American wars. This short exchange between these two women is a nice illustration of how the memory of the Civil War remained contested terrain a decade after Appomattox. See David Blight, *Race and Reunion: The Civil War in American Memory* (Cambridge: Harvard University Press, 2001).

14. Abby House (1797?–1881) was an ardent Confederate supporter who collected clothing and food for Southern soldiers and also nursed many back to health. Her gravestone reads: "Angel of Mercy to Confederate Soldiers."

15. A veteran of the Mexican-American War, the Virginian Gen. Joseph E. Johnston (1807–1891) served the Confederacy throughout the Civil War. Shortly after Lee's surrender at Appomattox Court House, Johnston surrendered the Army of Tennessee to Gen. William T. Sherman in central North Carolina.

16. Albert D. Richardson (1833–1869), a journalist for the *New York Daily Tribune* and spy for the Union army was taken prisoner by the Confederates at Vicksburg in 1863. Richardson was transferred to Salisbury prison in 1864, where he was assigned to remove the clothing from the Union dead. He and two other men managed to escape in 1865. Four years later Richardson became the victim in a celebrated murder case when Daniel McFarland gunned him down in the *Tribune* offices in a jealous rage over his ex-wife, actress Abby Sage McFarland.

17. Maj. John H. Gee was the commander of Salisbury prison from 1864 to 1865. After the war he was found not guilty in a military court on two counts of violating the law and customs of war. Dickinson had apparently also heard of the misdeeds of Sergeant Harris and Major Myers, the post commissary, but neither of these officers ever faced criminal charges. See Guénaël Mettraux, "A Little-known Case from the American Civil War: The War Crimes Trial of

Major General John H. Gee," *Journal of International Criminal Justice* 8.4 (September 2010): 1059–68.

18. Mrs. Sarah R. Johnston's efforts to assist the prisoners of war at Salisbury Prison earned her some postwar fame in the North. In their celebratory volume on wartime women, which Dickinson had almost certainly read, Linus Pierpont Brockett and Mary C. Vaughan devoted a short chapter to Johnston's efforts and the hostility she faced from her fellow North Carolinians. Dr. L. P. Brockett and Mrs. Mary C. Vaughan, *Woman's Work in the Civil War: A Record of Heroism, Patriotism, and Patience* (Philadelphia: Ziegler, McCurdy & Co., 1867), 269–72.

19. In 1865 General George Stoneman Jr. (1822–1894) commanded raids through Virginia and North Carolina, freeing roughly fourteen hundred Northern prisoners at Salisbury prison.

20. Dickinson is referring to a clipping she enclosed with the letter.

21. Dickinson was clearly describing Maj. Gen. Daniel Harvey Hill (1821–1889) and not "B. F. Hill." After his career in the Confederate army, Major General Hill settled in Charlotte, where he edited the highly influential literary and historical journal, *The Land We Love.* He later became the first president of the University of Arkansas.

22. Randolph Abbott Shotwell (1844–1885) served in the Confederate army and after the war became a prominent Charlotte editor and conservative political figure. In 1871 federal officials arrested him for his Ku Klux Klan activities. In the unidentifiable phrase it seems that Dickinson is using some satirical term for the KKK.

23. Dickinson is speaking of one of several African American members of the South Carolina state legislature.

24. The Mecklenburg Declaration of Independence, known as the nation's first declaration of independence, was signed in Charlotte in 1775. The legitimacy of this declaration has been hotly contested since in 1819, when it was first published.

25. The system of sharecropping became a dominant form of agricultural labor in the postwar south. Landowners, who lacked the cash to hire wage workers, contracted with independent farmers, who lacked the wealth to rent their own farms. In this world of

ample land and labor and scarce cash, the sharecropper agreed to work the land in exchange for a "share" of the profits from the sale of crops. In practice, sharecroppers were only rarely able to save enough money to purchase their own farms. Many, particularly poor black farmers, slipped into a form of debt peonage, where each year was a struggle to pay off the accumulated debts from the previous season. In this passage, Dickinson draws an important distinction between those farmers who were working their own land and the poorer sharecroppers.

26. Born in Massachusetts, a veteran of the Union army, Daniel Chamberlain (1835–1907) moved to South Carolina in 1866. He served as the Republican governor of South Carolina from 1874 to 1876. Chamberlain's wife, Alice, became a good friend.

27. A *tableau vivant* is the reenactment of a theatrical scene in which the "actors" stand frozen in a particular pose. Martha Washington tea parties were a popular fund-raising scheme in both the North and the South.

28. The term "waving the bloody shirt" refers to the postwar Republican strategy of invoking wartime bloodshed as a rhetorical tool against Democratic candidates. Here Dickinson is suggesting that the *New York Tribune,* which favored sectional reconciliation, would be unfairly critical of Mrs. Chamberlain's actions towards these hostile Southern women.

29. John C. Calhoun (1782–1850) was one of South Carolina's most celebrated antebellum politicians and a powerful voice for state's rights. George McDuffie (1790–1851) served as governor of South Carolina and as a U.S. senator.

30. The iron palmetto tree in front of the State House was created by Charleston ironworker Christopher Werner in 1858.

31. Henry Purvis was the son of the famous Philadelphia African American abolitionist Robert Purvis. Dickinson had grown up with Purvis's sister, and the Purvis family was the inspiration for the biracial family in Dickinson's 1868 novel *What Answer?*

Nashville, Tennessee

1. Opened in 1761, St. Michael's is the oldest church in Charleston.

2. Fort Sumter stands in Charleston Harbor. On April 12, 1861, Confederate forces in Charleston fired on the federal garrison at Fort Sumter, effectively starting the Civil War. Dickinson repeatedly misspelled the fort as "Sumpter."

3. Battery Wagner, also known as Fort Wagner, was a Confederate fortification on Morris Island, protecting the southern entrance to Charleston Harbor. Col. Robert Gould Shaw (1837–1863) commanded the all-black 54th Massachusetts Volunteer Infantry in their celebrated charge on Battery Wagner on July 18, 1863. Shaw, who was white, and a quarter of his men fell in the failed assault, which turned national attention on the heroism of the men in the U.S. Colored Troops. The 54th and the assault were depicted in the 1989 film *Glory*.

4. Here Dickinson is contrasting her responses to Fort Sumter and Battery Wagner.

5. When Colonel Shaw fell at Fort Wagner, the Confederates buried him in a common grave with his men. The Confederates meant to insult Shaw and his memory by burying the white officer with his black soldiers, but the Shaw family, deeply committed to abolitionism, considered it a point of honor that their son had been buried with his black troops and rejected any attempts to recover the body.

6. Dickinson, a frequent visitor to New York City, is comparing The Battery with New York's Fifth Avenue.

7. Runaway slaves often took refuge in the Georgia swampland.

8. Wright Square, laid out in 1733, was among the first squares in Savannah, Georgia. Today the square is flanked with monuments, a church and other landmarks. Franklin Square is one of Philadelphia's most grand squares.

9. New Haven, Connecticut, was celebrated for its streets lined with elm trees.

10. Col. Charles Olmstead (1837–1926) commanded Fort Pulaski, located in Savannah. Fort Pulaski fell to Union forces in April 1862, cutting off a crucial port and railway hub for the Confederacy.

11. Kazimierz Pułaski (1745–1779) was a Polish soldier who immigrated to the American colonies, where he fought with George

Washington in the American Revolution. General Pułaski fell at the Battle of Savannah.

12. In this sentence, Dickinson apparently meant "burden."

13. "Quadroon" refers to an individual who was one-quarter black.

14. Here the chambermaid was speaking of biracial children ("yellow" skinned) who were the product of the sexual abuse of slave women by their white owners.

15. Henry G. Worthington (1828–1909), born in Maryland, during the Civil War served as the first congressman from Nevada and later as well as minister to Uruguay and to the Argentine Republic.

16. During the Civil War, Clara Barton (1821–1912) served as a nurse, organizing medical supplies and aid to wounded soldiers. After President Lincoln put her in charge of the search for lost soldiers, Pvt. Dorence Atwater came to her with a list of soldiers who had died in Andersonville prison. When the war ended, Barton and Atwater went to Andersonville and placed hand-painted grave markers for each of the fallen soldiers.

Evansville, Indiana

1. The Hermitage Plantation, built by Henry McAlpin (1777–1851), featured "Savannah grey bricks," made from clay found on the property.

2. James Oglethorpe founded the colony of Georgia. The Yamacraw were a Native American tribe who were the first to settle the area that became Savannah.

3. The minister was speaking of "the Island of Patmos," but Dickinson's phonetic spelling here appears to be "Paramos."

4. In this section, as in earlier portions of the letters, Dickinson is attempting to convey—and perhaps mock—the African American dialects she had heard. Her unusual spelling and her difficult handwriting present particular challenges for transcription.

5. A native of Athens, Georgia, Capt. Henry Jackson (1820–1898) graduated from Yale College and served in the Mexican War and later as minister resident to the Austrian Empire. During the Civil War he fought for the Confederacy and rose to the rank of major general before being captured at Nashville. After the war he

was a railroad executive and banker. In 1875, the year of Dickinson's visit, he became president of the Georgia Historical Society.

6. A native of Savannah, Gen. Robert H. Anderson (1835–1888) graduated from the U.S. Military Academy in 1857. During the war, General Anderson fought for the Confederacy, rising to the rank of brigadier general. After the war he became the chief of police in Savannah, a position he held for twenty-one years.

7. On September 19–20, 1863, the Confederate Army of Tennessee, under Gen. Braxton Bragg, defeated the Army of the Cumberland, commanded by Maj. Gen. William Rosecrans, in the mountains of northwest Georgia, near Chickamagua Creek. Following the Battle of Chickamagua, one of the bloodiest engagements of the war, the Union army retreated to Chattanooga. Although the Confederate forces laid siege to Chattanooga, the Union army—now under the command of George H. Thomas—managed to remain supplied, thanks to the arrival of reinforcements and the assistance of Gen. Ulysses S. Grant.

On November 24, 1863, a portion of the Army of the Potomac, commanded by Joseph Hooker, defeated a strong Confederate position at Lookout Mountain. The following day, Grant routed Bragg at Missionary Ridge, avenging the defeat at Chickamagua and giving the Union control of the crucial region.

8. This is an altered version of the poem "The Place to Die" (1840) by Irish poet Michael J. Barry. The original poem reads "Whether on the scaffold high."

9. Fisk University, named for Clinton B. Fisk of the Tennessee Freedmen's Bureau, was founded in 1866 as an institution of higher learning for African Americans. Vanderbilt University was established in 1873 from a $1 million endowment given by Cdr. Cornelius Vanderbilt.

10. Oberlin College (Ohio) was opened in 1835, and two years later it began accepting black students. In 1867 the college opened a music division.

11. The lynching victim was named Joe Reed. The policeman, Robert Frazier, was a Confederate veteran and apparently the first Nashville policeman to be killed on duty.

12. The convict leasing system was created after the Civil War to address the shortage of labor in the South after the emancipation

of slaves. The state would lease the prisoners and their labor to private companies for a specified fee, without compensating the prisoners for the work. This practice often took on a racial cast, as black convicts found themselves disproportionately sent off to work on chain gangs, while whites remained in the penitentiaries.

13. Gen. Galusha Pennypacker (1844–1916), a Medal of Honor recipient for his heroism at Fort Fisher, was promoted to brigadier general in 1865 at the age of twenty, making him the youngest officer to hold that rank.

14. On several occasions in her career, Dickinson worked herself into complete exhaustion, forcing her to seek medical attention.

15. "Dickey" was Dickinson's sister, Susan. Julia was probably her friend Julia Gould.

Suggested Reading

Andrews, Sidney. *The South since the War: As Shown by Fourteen Weeks of Travel and Observation in Georgia and the Carolinas.* Edited by Heather Cox Richardson. 1866. Reprint, Baton Rouge: Louisiana State University Press, 2004.

Ayers, Edward L. *The Promise of the New South: Life after Reconstruction.* New York: Oxford University Press, 1992.

Blight, David W. *Race and Reunion: The Civil War in American Memory.* Cambridge, Mass.: Belknap Press of Harvard University Press, 2001.

Bode, Carl. *The American Lyceum: Town Meeting of the Mind.* New York: Oxford University Press, 1956.

Dickinson, Anna E. *A Paying Investment.* Boston: R. Osgood and Company, 1876.

———. *A Ragged Register (of People, Places, and Opinions).* New York: Harper & Brothers, 1879.

———. *What Answer?* 1868. Reprint, Amherst, N.Y.: Humanity Books, 2003.

Edwards, Laura F. *Gendered Strife and Confusion: The Political Culture of Reconstruction.* Urbana: University of Illinois Press, 1997.

Faulkner, Carol. *Women's Radical Reconstruction: The Freedmen's Aid Movement.* Philadelphia: University of Pennsylvania Press, 2004.

Fitzgerald, Michael W. *Splendid Failure: Postwar Reconstruction in the South.* Chicago: Ivan R. Dee, 2007.

Foner, Eric. *Reconstruction: America's Unfinished Revolution, 1863–1877.* New York: Harper & Row, 1988.

Gallman, J. Matthew. *America's Joan of Arc: The Life of Anna Elizabeth Dickinson.* New York: Oxford University Press, 2006.

———. "Anna Dickinson, America's Joan of Arc: Public Discourse and Gendered Rhetoric during the Civil War." In *American Public Life and the Historical Imagination,* edited by Wendy Gamber,

Michael Grossberg, and Hendrik Hartog. Notre Dame, Ind.: University of Notre Dame Press, 2003.

———. "Is the War Ended? Anna Dickinson and the Election of 1872." In *The Memory of the Civil War in American Culture,* edited by Alice Fahs and Joan Waugh. Chapel Hill: University of North Carolina Press, 2004.

———. *Northerners at War: Reflections on the Civil War Home Front.* Kent, Ohio: Kent State University Press, 2010.

Hahn, Steven. *A Nation under Our Feet: Black Struggles in the Rural South from Slavery to the Great Migration.* Cambridge: Harvard University Press, 2003.

Hunter, Tera W. *To 'Joy My Freedom: Southern Black Women's Lives and Labors after the Civil War.* Cambridge, Mass.: Harvard University Press, 1997.

Janney, Caroline. *Burying the Dead but Not the Past: Ladies' Memorial Associations and the Lost Cause.* Chapel Hill: University of North Carolina Press, 2007.

Kelley, Mary. *Learning to Stand and Speak: Women, Education, and Public Life in America's Republic.* Chapel Hill: Published for the Omohundro Institute of Early American History and Culture, Williamsburg, Virginia, by the University of North Carolina Press, 2006.

———. *Private Woman, Public Stage: Literary Domesticity in Nineteenth-Century America.* Chapel Hill: University of North Carolina Press, 2002.

Martineau, Harriet. *Society in America.* 1837. Reprint, Garden City, N.Y.: Anchor Books, 1962.

McPherson, James M. "Abolitionists and the Civil Rights Act of 1875." *Journal of American History* 52 (December 1965): 483–510.

Olmsted, Frederick Law. *The Cotton Kingdom: A Traveller's Observations on Cotton and Slavery in the American Slave States: Based upon Three Former Volumes of Journeys and Investigations by the Same Author.* Edited by Arthur M. Schlesinger. Reprint, New York: Modern Library, 1984.

Ransom, Roger L., and Richard Sutch. *One Kind of Freedom: The Economic Consequences of Emancipation.* Second ed. New York: Cambridge University Press, 2001.

Ray, Angela G. *The Lyceum and Public Culture in the Nineteenth-Century United States.* East Lansing: Michigan State University Press, 2005.

Reid, Whitelaw. *After the War: A Tour of the Southern States, 1865–1866.* Edited by C. Vann Woodward. New York: Harper & Row, 1965.

Richardson, Heather Cox. *The Death of Reconstruction: Race, Labor, and Politics in the Post-Civil War North, 1865–1901.* Cambridge, Mass.: Harvard University Press, 2001.

———. *West from Appomattox: The Reconstruction of America after the Civil War.* New Haven: Yale University Press, 2007.

Robison, Lori. "'Writing Reconstruction': Race and Visualist Ideology in Whitelaw Reid's *After the War.*" *Journal of Narrative Theory* 29 (Winter 1999): 85–109.

Schwalm, Leslie A. *A Hard Fight for We: Women's Transition from Slavery to Freedom in South Carolina.* Urbana: University of Illinois Press, 1997.

Scott, Anne Firor. *The Southern Lady: From Pedestal to Politics, 1830–1930.* Chicago: University of Chicago Press, 1970.

Silber, Nina. *The Romance of Reunion: Northerners and the South, 1865–1890.* Chapel Hill: University of North Carolina Press, 1993.

Slap, Andrew L. *The Doom of Reconstruction: The Liberal Republicans in the Civil War Era.* New York: Fordham University Press, 2006.

Tocqueville, Alexis de. *Democracy in America.* Translation by Arthur Goldhammer. New York: Library of America, 2004.

Trowbridge, John Townsend. *The Desolate South, 1865–1866: A Picture of the Battlefields and of the Devastated Confederacy.* Freeport, N.Y.: Books for Libraries Press, 1970.

Varon, Elizabeth. *Southern Lady, Yankee Spy: The True Story of Elizabeth Van Lew.* New York: Oxford University Press, 2003.

Whites, LeeAnn. *Gender Matters: Civil War, Reconstruction, and the Making of the New South.* New York: Palgrave Macmillan, 2005.

Index

INDEX

INDEX

INDEX

CPSIA information can be obtained at www.ICGtesting.com
Printed in the USA
BVOW031101141011
273489BV00002B/2/P

9 780813 134246